GIVE US YOUR SICK

GIVE US YOUR SICK

An Exploration of Immigrant Small Business Owners' Health Care Acquisition Journeys

ARIANNA KOHILAKIS

GIVE US YOUR SICK
AN EXPLORATION OF IMMIGRANT SMALL BUSINESS OWNERS' HEALTH CARE ACQUISITION JOURNEYS

iUniverse books may be ordered through booksellers or by contacting:

iUniverse
1663 Liberty Drive
Bloomington, IN 47403
www.iuniverse.com
844-349-9409

ISBN: 978-1-6632-1063-0 (sc)
ISBN: 978-1-6632-1062-3 (e)

Library of Congress Control Number: 2020919457

Print information available on the last page.

iUniverse rev. date: 11/03/2020

CONTENTS

CHAPTER 1

INTRODUCTION

As I sit writing this overlooking the canals of Amsterdam, I am reminded of the differences between each and every country. The opportunity to travel to many countries has opened my eyes to the differences in each society. I see the variability of the lifestyle, the fashion and the cuisine. I enjoy the differences in each culture and have come to appreciate that while there are vast differences in the people, we all share the same basic needs. The need for human interaction, for nourishment, and, as this book will attempt to understand, for health care.

When my Papou—the Greek word for grandfather—emigrated from Greece in 1948 at the age of 18 and came to the US, he was first stationed in Alaska. They took an immigrant from the islands of Greece, stationed him in the northernmost state of the United States and—after seeing his inability in the kitchen, as was inferred by his blatantly Greek last name— gave him the role of a ski instructor.

Nearly 66 years later, I had the opportunity to smell the same pure, Alaskan air that greeted his nose (which was accustomed to the salty, dry heat of Crete). Visiting the station with my Papou, I realized the courage that his journey took. Not only did he come to a country where he hardly spoke the language, had no family, and had a completely different lifestyle from that he had grown accustomed to; he left behind a country where he was raised, a country where had every comfort he could imagine, a country for which he had just fought in a civil war. My Papou's unrelenting drive to succeed in America is undoubtedly my predominant inspiration, but the most amazing part is that there are millions of immigrants with stories with even more amazing plots, people whom I have walked past on the street in New York City or sat next to in my lectures at Cornell.

While he is no longer with us, Papou has deeply inspired this book. But not just *my* Papou. As I sit around the table with my big fat Greek family at Thanksgiving, a quarter of the smiles that greet me belong to immigrants. As I stand at the services at my church, I overlook the heads of countless immigrants who made the same trek as my Papou. In each corner of my life, I am able to identify immigrants who have paved the way before me.

This book is inspired by the millions of immigrants who have uprooted their lives and planted themselves in the United States despite every reason not to. It is dedicated to all of the brave people who continue to approach immigration as an opportunity to sow a new seed in a new land, with the hope of growing that seed into future generations, like myself.

This book is not going to focus on my Papou, because while he no doubt could fill each and every page, he faced a problem different than those faced today. He was not a small business owner. He was not someone who was pitted against a system that purposefully makes it extremely difficult to succeed due to limited resources and an abundance of cultural and social barriers.

I decided to write this book because immigrants deserve a synthesized collection of their stories. So, rather than appreciating isolated success stories, we, the American public, can truly appreciate the magnitude of their success. Not just on their own, but as complete units.

In a time when these groups are revitalizing an economy threatened by stagnation, it is essential to appreciate the contributions of these pivotal groups. Furthermore, in a political climate divided by the debate on immigration, this population is under the magnifying glass more than ever before. Understanding their potential relative to any threats as early and as accurately as possible is valuable in drafting legislation.

The power of immigrant households in keeping the American economy afloat is paramount to the success of our country. According to the Fiscal Policy Institute (FPI), immigrants make up 18% of small business owners nationwide. Small businesses employed 4.7 million people in 2010, and immigrants are found to have both business formation and ownership rates when compared to non-immigrants. According to the Minority Business

Development Agency of the U.S. Department of Commerce, "roughly one out of ten immigrant workers owns a business and 620 of 100,000 immigrants (0.62 percent) start a business each month" (MBDA). This book is not one of statistics, yet I believe the inclusion of these numbers is necessary to underscore what an integral part of the American economy small businesses comprise. Rather, this is a book of stories. Those of success. Those of failure. And those of people still working towards making it on their own.

Before delving into the stories of small business owners from immigrant backgrounds, we must first understand the factors that have created a health care climate where health insurance acquisition has become extremely complex. A *New York Times* opinion piece, "How to Fix a Broken Health Care System," was written in late December 2018, and compiled a series of letters sent by readers to the editor. One contributor, Isabella Vitti of Brooklyn, shared:

> "I am fortunate enough to have decent health insurance
> through my employer. However, this means that if I want
> to switch jobs, for a better salary or a job that better
> suits my career goals, I may have to go without health
> insurance for a risky period of time, or pay the exorbitant
> Cobra costs. I would also be more hesitant to work for a
> small company that may not provide health insurance.
> Wouldn't we be served better if people could pursue their
> careers without having to worry about having employer
> health insurance coverage?"

This opinion is by no means an isolated idea. This book will walk us through the nuances and complexities of the American health care system that immigrants must face. This factual background is interwoven with stories told in the voices of these business owners themselves, which will bring readers one step closer to understanding a system overlooked by so many.

I hope that these words—which have been composed as a result of my deep-rooted passion and interest in immigrant small businesses and health care—will teach, excite, motivate and contribute to your personal intellectual growth on these topics.

CHAPTER 2

HEALTH CARE BACKGROUND

In order to truly understand what these small business owners are faced with, we must understand the current health care system in the United States. Officially known as H.R. 3962, the Affordable Health Care for America Act was originally passed in May of 2010. It has since been modified and certain portions have been repealed. It is the predominant health care legislation in the United States. Often referred to as Obamacare or the ACA, the bill has been extremely contentious due to the wider implications of deepening government involvement in public health care provision. Within the ACA—a 1990-page bill—certain sections pertain specifically to small businesses. This direct regulation on small business health care operations led to a widespread push to educate small business owners on what was newly expected of them by the government in order to minimize any penalties and further economic strife for their businesses.

The two key mandates are the employer mandate and the individual mandate. According to resources provided by the U.S. Chamber of Commerce, the employer mandate essentially states that businesses with fifty or more "full-time equivalent" employees (FTEs) are required to offer a certain level of health coverage to employees to avoid owing a tax penalty. According to the IRS, an FTE is, "for a calendar month, an employee employed on average at least 30 hours of service per week, or 130 hours of service per month" (IRSFTE). The employer mandate stunts business growth in two main ways. The first is that some small businesses try to stay below the threshold of fifty full-time equivalent employees in order to avoid penalization for not offering health care. The second is that once the penalty is triggered, its size varies based on the number of FTEs, further discouraging the growth of small businesses. The individual mandate, recently repealed in December of 2017, also had implications on small businesses, though less directly. The individual mandate required that every individual person obtain health care or face a tax penalty. Though the individual mandate does not speak directly to small business employees, many of those working for small businesses who do not qualify for the benefits of full-time employment through the company were affected by the new legislation. Both mandates prompted widespread reconsideration within small businesses and encouraged their owners to acquaint themselves with the new health care to respond in the best interests of their employees and businesses.

Offering health care to employees has a range of benefits. Various reports have indicated that health insurance is the most valued employee benefit. According to the CDC, offering health care is also associated with increased employee productivity (CDCWP) and employee satisfaction. Furthermore, the premise of a group-purchased health care plan facilitates access to a wider range of hospitals and doctors than is attainable with most individual network plans. So, even though the individual mandate is no longer in place, it is in everyone's best interests to take a collective approach to health care. Additionally, there are monetary savings for both employees and employers. Employer contributions to health care are tax-deductible whereas employees buying health insurance on their own are forced to use post-tax dollars to buy it. In businesses that offer group health insurance, employee compensation premiums have potential to be reduced and "employer payroll taxes are reduced by 7.65 percent of employee contributions" (IRSTT).

Acknowledging the challenging and time-consuming nature of researching the ideal health insurance plan for each company, the government tried to simplify the process with the creation of the Small Business Health Options Program (SHOP). SHOP was established for small employers—with the working definition of 1-to-50 full-time equivalent employees—looking to provide their employees with health and dental coverage. While SHOP has many benefits, it also restricts small businesses in that to qualify for the Small Business Health Care Tax Credit (which lowers astronomical premium costs) small businesses must get their insurance through a SHOP-registered agent or broker. This impedes their ability to utilize private insurance companies and creates an overall less-competitive health insurance market.

There are seven key ACA requirements that pertain directly to small business owners. Learning what is being asked of these small business owners is fundamental to understanding their decisions and to formulate improved policy options. The first requirement is that employers report general information about the insurance marketplace to their employees, regardless of whether or not the employer offers health insurance. The second requirement consists of disclosure rules that require employers to provide employees with a Summary of Benefits and Coverage (SBC) form that explains exactly what their health plan covers and what it costs. The next requirement puts specific regulations on the Flexible Spending Accounts, or FSAs. FSAs are arrangements through which employees can use tax-free dollars to pay a certain amount of out-of-pocket medical expenses that may arise. The regulations pertain to employers setting limits to how much money can be put in the FSA and therefore exempted from tax, how long money can remain in the FSA, and how carrying over between annual plans functions. The fourth requirement is the implementation of "Workplace Wellness Programs" in which the government incentivizes healthier workplaces by contributing a percentage—currently 30%—towards the cost of health care coverage with successful program creation. The fifth requirement institutes a ninety-day maximum waiting period between the time that an employee is hired and when they are offered insurance through their employer. The sixth requirement pertains to general reporting of information on health coverage by both employers and insurance companies. Every employer with fifty or more full-time employees (or self-insuring employer regardless of size) must report the health coverage they provide to their employees. The seventh and final requirement involves medical loss ratio rebates. If insurance companies fail to spend a minimum of 80% of premium dollars on medical care, they must provide a rebate to customers. As a means of enforcing these requirements, there are penalties for noncompliance. Small business owners must ensure each of these seven requirements in terms of health care for their employees. Rather than managing their employees as they see fit, there is a legal standard to which they are bound; failure to comply with these regulations results in economic implications that can seriously damage the growth of a small business.

Policymakers have acknowledged the difficulty for small businesses to satisfy the wide scope of requirements the ACA puts forth by incentivizing small business owners with tax credits. Qualifying for the "Small Business Health Care Tax Credit" consists of having less than twenty-five full-time equivalent employees, an average employee salary of less than $50,000 annually, employers pay at least 50% of employees' premium costs, and offering SHOP coverage to all full-time employees. Additionally, the tax credit is graduated in the sense that smaller businesses receive larger benefits. For those with less than ten employees who make annual salaries of less than $25,000, the credit is larger.

This tax graduation is another multi-sided issue within health care. While it is rational that smaller businesses would need more government help in order to succeed, especially when they are of such a minuscule size competing against businesses already established in particular market niches, the graduated tax credit can also be evaluated from the other side. Various small business owners have said that they stop hiring when they hit the mark of fifty employees because past that point the requirements under the ACA change for the business and owners feel unequipped to handle these changes. In essence, these tax credit rules almost function to discourage the growth of small businesses into larger and more self-sustainable companies, motivating them to rely on the crutch of a higher tax credit. Reinforcing small businesses to depend on the government weakens a significant portion of the economy, limiting the creation of new American jobs and the reduction of the national unemployment rate.

There are paragraphs upon paragraphs of fine print for all of these existing policies and ACA clauses, but understanding these general requirements gives a better sense as to the complexity of what is being asked of small business owners in today's health care climate.

Additionally, we must examine how bidding for health care functions and why it has been able to help small business owners. Acquiring health insurance is not as simple as walking into a grocery store, filling a cart with everything your employees need, and then paying at the cash register. The concept of competitive bidding has some central attractive features when executed properly: it creates an open, fair, and transparent environment, and any company regardless of size, revenue, or other potentially exclusive criteria is welcome to participate in the bidding processes. Often, health care bidding is done in a reverse auction format in which the seller sets an initially high price and subsequently drops it depending on the buyer's submissions.

Small business is a relative term. Wal-Mart employs over 2.3 million people internationally, whereas Starbucks only has approximately 254,000 employees. Neither business would be considered "small," but relative to Wal-Mart, Starbucks has over one-hundred times fewer employees, a mere 0.1104%. When utilizing the working definition of a business with 50 FTEs in 2014, CNN found that there are about 5.5 million "small businesses" in the United States. Immigrants in particular make up a substantial portion of small business owners—the Fiscal Policy Institute's Immigration Research Initiative indicates that more than one in six small business owners in the United States is an immigrant. Interestingly, a recent Brookings article stated that about half of Fortune 500 companies were founded by American immigrants or their children.

CHAPTER 3

EXPLANATION OF HEALTH CARE OPTIONS

Immigrants and their families are faced with a unique health care acquisition process. The majority of U.S. citizens, U.S. nationals, and lawfully present immigrants are eligible for coverage through the traditional United States Health Insurance Marketplace. As a note, undocumented immigrants—though not eligible to purchase marketplace health coverage or receive tax credits or other plan-based savings—are able to apply for coverage on the behalf of documented individuals. Even for those immigrants who qualify for marketplace insurance as members of the aforementioned groups, the actual process of deciding which health care plan will most efficiently and effectively cover employees' needs can be much more complicated.

A largely cited problem—as mentioned by small business owner Kateri Gutierrez in my conversation with her for this book—is the difficulty understanding how to enroll in programs. She explained that had she not taken personal finance courses nor been a member of such a technologically adept generation, she would have been unable to acquire health care for herself when she was not covered by her job as a substitute teacher. Increasing the transparency around health care has been an ongoing goal of policymakers and insurers.

As with any issue atop the political agenda, legislative changes affect different groups of people differently. For health care, the ACA was the central effort by the Obama administration. Since President Trump's time in office, the dismemberment of Obamacare—such as the elimination of the individual mandate—has had a mixed reception in corporate America. One website, Small Business Trends, which contains blog-like posts from business owners on a range of topics, spoke to small business owners to gauge the reception of current health policy. A post by the founder and CEO explained that there is a divide amongst those who liked the ACA and those who prefer the Trump Administration's changes. Small business owners who benefited from Obamacare cited their ability to get affordable coverage for pre-existing conditions and financial benefits from the subsidized rates. On the other hand, there is a population of business people who felt "disrupted and squeezed out of their old plans" (SBT) and had fewer health plan choices. These same business owners explained that they faced higher rates and larger deductibles when forced to purchase coverage on the ACA marketplace.

Prior to diving into the logistics of finding and acquiring health care as a small business owner, it is helpful to learn about the options available to them. For the purposes of this book, we will explore five options that have consistently been among the most popular benefits for small businesses over the past ten years (People Keep).

Traditional Group Health Insurance

The first of such plans is a traditional group health insurance plan, which consists of small businesses selecting a group plan to offer to employees (and potentially their dependents). The small business pays a fixed premium cost for the policy, a portion of which is often paid by the employees. Employees are additionally responsible for using their income for copays and deductibles associated with their use of services through the plan.

A benefit of the traditional plan is that employees are generally familiar with how it functions and, considerations of price-effectiveness aside, they are easy to obtain relative to alternatives. Coverage can usually be purchased through the government-run Small Business Health Options (SHOP) marketplaces or through private insurance brokers—though there is a tax subsidy if it is purchased in the SHOP marketplace offered by the government to encourage SHOP use.

The largest difficulty with traditional plans is that premium prices tend to make it extremely difficult for small businesses to afford this form of health care in tandem to all the other expenses they must pay. Mercer's National Survey on Benefit Trends cited that for small businesses (defined in this study as 500 employees or less), the cost of traditional group health insurance is estimated to be $13,363 per employee family in 2019.

Further, despite the seemingly simplistic nature of this plan—and even the misleading nomenclature of "SHOP," which suggests ease of selection and within the marketplace—only 29% of businesses with less than 50 employees offered group health plans in 2016 (according to NFIB).

QSEHRAs

Another type of benefit plan is the qualified small employer health reimbursement arrangements, known for short as QSEHRAs. Unlike more traditional plans which are structured to actually provide the health insurance, this is a less aggressive approach that instead subsidizes health costs incurred by small business employees. Essentially, QSEHRAs enable small employers of fewer than 50 full-time employees to reimburse employees for health insurance premiums and any other eligible medical expenses using tax-free dollars. The structure is fairly straightforward:

1. Employers design their plan and set reimbursement allowance amounts.
2. Employees select and pay for their own health insurance plans (including premiums and medical bills) to insurance companies and medical providers directly.
3. Employees provide proof of their expenses and submit a claim for expense reimbursement.
4. Employers reimburse employees with tax-free dollars up to the predetermined limit.

Unlike a bank account, the money is not given from employer to employee until a claim which qualifies for reimbursement is properly submitted and received (Command). The Internal Revenue Service regulates and has outlined eligibility for both employers and employees, which ensures the legality of the use of these tax-free dollars. For example, employees must provide proof of coverage of a health insurance plan that meets the Minimum Essential Coverage (MEC) Standards. The employees also must notify their marketplace or healthcare.gov of the QSHERA benefit received. There are also regulations on contribution amounts; for instance, the employer must be the sole funder and employers must adhere to annual maximum contribution amounts specific to self-only versus family coverage. Finally, there are rules for written notice that specify when and how the employer must notify eligible or ineligible employees of participation in QSEHRA (Command). The largest benefit of this plan is that employers can contribute to health insurance with tax-free dollars without having the same administrative responsibility and hassle of organizing and offering traditional group plans. Another reason for the popularity of QSEHRAs is that employees can choose the particular plan they want, as opposed to less personalized, one-size-fits-all plans.

While there are many benefits to QSEHRAs, there are also a few features that employees and employers should be aware of. For example, while all full-time employees must be equally included for reimbursement, employers have the choice to include or exclude part-time and seasonal employees. Another of such characteristics is the effect that the QSHERA reimbursement can have on tax credits already being received by employees prior to participation in the benefit plan. For employees who qualify for large credits on the individual market, their participation in a QSEHRA would offset government-provided tax credits. So rather than stacking benefits from a QSEHRA and the government to create an even larger tax credit, it would just result in a deduction from the government tax credit for the amount of the employer reimbursement.

Self-Funded Health Insurance

The third type of benefit plan is self-funded health insurance. Rather than purchasing the aforementioned traditional insurance, businesses have the alternative option of self-funding their own health care plan. In self-funding, the business is responsible for establishing a network of providers, making claims for incurred payments and collecting premiums from employees. Often, employers hire third-party administrators (TPAs) tasked with completing the above three duties to minimize the resource burden on the business itself, which arises when they decide to run a health care plan in addition to day-to-day operations. Additionally, when small firms engage in self-funding they are likely to buy stop-loss insurance. This insurance can be focused on aggregate health care costs or for specific employees who are recipients of particularly expensive treatments. Small firms are more likely to use this stop-loss insurance to complement their self-funded plan because they lack the "diversified employee base" or financial resources to absorb large overruns in health care expenses like large businesses. With the integration of TPAs and stop-loss insurance into self-funded plans, they might lose their purpose of cutting out third-party intermediaries, such as insurance companies. Yet, aside from the obvious risk of a company absorbing the health risks of their employees rather than deferring them to an insurance company, there are other benefits and obstacles associated with self-funding. One such benefit is the lower premium cost—estimated by the Brookings Institution to have relative costs savings estimated at 10 to 25 percent (according to the Self Insurance Educational Foundation), which is possible by cutting out the external marketing costs and profit margins of traditional health insurance. Another is the greater flexibility in designing benefit packages.

With self-funding, it is extremely important to keep up to date with changes in legislation. With the ACA, there were many regulatory incentives for self-funding. Many of the new provisions (which were obstacles for other types of health insurance) had loopholes for self-funding. For example, while the "bans on pre-existing condition denials" and annual caps applied to both self-funded and traditional health insurance, there were other areas where small firms could avoid significant ACA and state requirements if they chose self-funding. Self-funded plans are not subject to the community rating requirement (which restricts how insurers can use health factors such as age and smoking status to calculate total premiums charged to the firm), the Essential Health Benefit (or EHB, which stipulates that minimum coverage for health care plans sold by insurers to small firms must include maternity care, mental health, and preventative services), medical loss ratio requirements (which mandate a certain percentage of funds—80%—be allocated to health care activities compared to for administrative functions), the health insurance tax (a

2% federal tax in 2014 on most health care premiums), and the state taxes (roughly 1.75% the premiums in 2014). Of course, not all of these requirements help the employees as much as the small business itself, as the minimized role of government in regulating health care gives more discretion to the owner of the small business.

According to the Brookings Institution, a mere 8 to 16 percent of firms with less than 100 FTEs self-fund their health care plans (BROOKINGS). Self-funding is much more popular at larger (i.e., greater than 1,000 FTEs) firms because they are much less likely to be adversely affected by large numbers of claims.

Integrated Health Reimbursement Arrangement (IHRA) (PKIHRA)

Alternatively, group-integrated HRAs are another option available for small business owners. Integrated HRAs are only offered to employees who take part in group health insurance. A Health Reimbursement Arrangement (HRA) is an IRS-approved, employer-funded medical expense reimbursement plan. Just as in a QSEHRA, the employer is allowed to reimburse employees with tax-free dollars for individual health insurance premiums and eligible medical expenses. The integrated portion of this plan is that the employer-funded medical reimbursement plan is directly linked with a group health insurance plan. Oftentimes, the plan is high-deductible (where the deductible is much higher relative to the premiums). It is not uncommon for a company to sponsor a group health insurance plan with the higher deductible but same coverage so that they can have savings with the lower premiums. Then the company likely will offer the integrated HRA to cover the difference between the original deductible and the high deductible of the new insurance plan. Employees then use the integrated HRA to be reimbursed for out-of-pocket medical expenses. Due to the fact that the integrated HRA is a supplement to help employees with their deductible costs, it is only available to those who take part in the group health insurance plan of the company. Depending on the plan, companies usually realize about 30-50% in savings when an integrated HRA is put into place (according to People Keep).

The outcomes and implications of HRAs are relatively new due to the fact that they were only recently directly mentioned in legislation. HRAs are not explicitly mentioned in the Affordable Care Act and were not formally recognized in the tax code before 2016. President Trump directed the Departments of Health and Human Services, Labor, and Treasury to "increase the usability of HRAs, to expand employers' ability to offer HRAs to their employees, and to allow HRAs to be used in conjunction with non-group coverage" (HAT) in an executive order from October 2017.

Association Health Plans

The final benefit plan—and perhaps the most revolutionary in terms of cost savings—are Association Health Plans. In conversation with many small business owners, a commonly felt restraint when approaching health care is that their business is too small to negotiate a desirable health care package. Association Health Plans answer this difficulty for small businesses by enabling small businesses to unite with other businesses when purchasing health insurance plans (AHPSB). The larger groups are able to offer plans together that meet certain rules. The benefit of banding together when acquiring health care is that insurance risk is then spread out over a larger pool of people. This, in turn, leads to health coverage at a lesser cost than when the risk was more concentrated at a single small business.

A new rule issued by the Department of Labor in June 2018 and made effective September 1, 2018, expanded the accessibility to Associations Health Plans (AHPs) for small businesses. In the comments received by the Department of Labor before passing the new rule, it was said that small business owners were "very supportive" (AHPSB) of the rule as an opportunity to "expand the options they have to obtain more affordable health care coverage for themselves and their employees" (PPACA). Rather than limiting participation to businesses with a minimum of 50 full-time employees, small businesses with as few as one employee are eligible for association health plans. Now, these businesses are able to shop for and join association health plans they were previously blocked from. Additionally, the new rule creates for association health plans with expanded consumer protections, such as pre-existing conditions coverage. Another change included in this new rule is that association health plans can now cross borders, allowing for the formation of nationwide groups under a single plan.

There are a variety of risks and costs which have been found to be related to AHPs, particularly without the federal regulatory standards of the Affordable Care Act to regulate them. One such risk is that of discriminatory coverage based on gender, age, or industry. Whereas the Affordable Care Act prevented insurers from changing premiums or levels of coverage dependent on these characteristics, the new regulations are easier to circumvent. Additionally, association plans were previously required to pay at least 60 percent of average medical costs and cover "essential health benefits" such as maternity and mental health care. The new rule does not require the same depth of coverage in these areas as the ACA before it. Two other concerns are high rates of fraud and mismanagement. The apprehension surrounding potential fraud is that lowering the barriers to form AHPs will make it easier for people or groups to use the plans as a front for fraud by creating AHPs as scams. Furthermore, the effective management of these plans is a potential issue due to the lack of prior experience in offering health insurance possessed in newly formed groups (EHI).

While this chapter has been largely informational, this is the material that we as readers and small business owners must understand when approaching the current health care acquisition environment. The statistics serve to show the range of options and variations among the needs and capacities of each business. So much of the uncertainty in selecting the best health care plan for a given business arises from being unaware of the range of options available—especially the more out-of-the-box methods. Similarly, those who have heard fragmented information about less conventional plans are less inclined to offer the hard-earned profits of themselves and their employees towards payments they are uncertain about, thereby ruling out many of the nontraditional options. Of these five explanations, understanding the legal foundation and relative pros and cons holds to be just as valuable as considering the logistical aspect of getting such a benefit plan.

CHAPTER 4

VALUE OF IMMIGRANT SMALL BUSINESS OWNERS TO THE ECONOMY

Immigrant small business owners occupy an important niche within their communities, one that cannot be easily filled by large corporations. There is an intimate nature of the interactions between small business owners and community members, which is further amplified in immigrants who are making new homes for themselves and their families in their new communities. Often, the establishment of the families of immigrants to America is very dependent on their home community and how they are welcomed by new neighbors with whom they often do not share a culture, language, or religion.

Given the intertwined nature of immigrant and non-immigrant business interactions, it is difficult to definitively identify the direct impact of immigration on the United States economy. But one thing is clear: supporting immigrant entrepreneurs is more than an act of charity. It is a justifiable strategy to bring the United States economy closer to economic growth. Research from the National Academies of Sciences, Engineering, and Medicine found that "the fiscal impacts of immigrants are generally positive at the federal level and generally negative at the state and local level" (NASEM) over a 75-year period of time (VOX). Furthermore, the same study found that, overall, immigrants are contributing more in payments to the federal government in the form of taxes than they receive in benefits. However, the opposite was found to be true for state and local governments, which were found to pay more benefits to immigrants than they paid in. This is largely attributed to the cost of educating incoming immigrant children. Yet, despite costs in some areas, the understanding that immigrant-owned businesses have made tremendous contributions to the U.S. economy persists. As a New York Times article explained, "Immigrants have high business formation rates, and many of the businesses they create are very successful, hire employees, and export goods and services to other countries" (SBAG).

In a paper published by the Harvard Business School written by researchers Sari Pekkala Kerr and William R. Kerr, the Survey of Business Owners (SBO) data from 2007 and 2012 was used to study both immigrant entrepreneurship and firm ownership. This particular study quantifies the dependency of the United States on the contributions of immigrant entrepreneurs in terms of firm formation and job creation. "First-generation immigrants create about 25% of new firms in the United States, but this share exceeds 40% in some states." Additionally, this research evaluated the types of businesses started by immigrants and the quality of the jobs created by their firms to best understand the value of what immigrants are contributing to the United States. It was found that immigrant-owned firms pay comparable wages to native-owned firms. An interesting finding of the same study was that despite the competitive wage offerings, immigrant-owned firms are less likely to offer benefits to their employees than American native-owned firms (IEAHBS). Data from the Survey of Business Owners and the American Community Survey (CENSUS) found 18 percent of firms with fewer than 100 full-time employees are immigrant-owned, more than the 13 percent of immigrant-owned total national firms. Since 1990, the share of small businesses in the United States owned by immigrants has increased by fifty percent (NYT).

Experts on the topic of immigration have identified a fragmented public response to the issue. The executive director for the New American Economy advocacy group, Jeremy Robbins, has attempted to clarify certain points in the media. "Immigration is top of the agenda politically, but the national discussion often bears little resemblance to the facts on the ground," said Robbins. "In community after community and industry after industry, immigration is helping America and American workers" (POLI). As David Dyssegaard Kallick, who authored the report, told BusinessWeek:

> "The conversation around immigrants' role in the economy is often dominated by two oversimplified ideas… Immigrants are either seen as strictly in competition with native-born workers for jobs, or immigration is seen as a magic bullet to revive stagnant economies. While the impact of immigrants on job growth can be overstated… people sometimes don't realize that when immigrants come into the economy, the economy also grows. Beyond statistics, immigrants are producing tangible benefits to the communities they have grown in" (BW).

The detriment of making blanket statements (and seeking blanket coverage) has become clear through our previous critiques of health insurance acquisition; the same ideas apply to the critical analyses of how immigrant entrepreneurs are valued in each state. Many factors go into how a person chooses which state to settle in, with some pursuing geographic convenience and others more consciously seeking a socioeconomic ecosystem that will allow their business idea to thrive. As expected, in immigration "gateway" states such as California, more than 40% of new firms have at least one or more immigrant owners. Contrarily, in a state such as Idaho or North Dakota, the share is less than 5%. The research becomes even more interesting when it reveals that job creation rates closely resemble firm creation rates. Immigrant-owned firms are more likely to survive and have been found to grow at a faster pace than native-owned firms over the four year time period from 2007 to 2011. Statistics such as this one begin to speak to the long-run importance of encouraging entrepreneurs to immigrate to the United States.

Aside from the creation of jobs, there is another notable characteristic of immigrant-owned firms that has been supported by existing research: innovation. Brown et al. in 2018 utilized data from the Census Bureau's 2014 Annual Survey of Entrepreneurs to evaluate the innovative behavior between immigrant- and native-owned firms (BROWN). For 24 of 26 measures (the two outliers being copyrights and trademarks), researchers found higher rates of innovation in immigrant-owned firms. This held true regardless of the age of the firm and the education level of its founders. "The data imply a robust immigrant advantage in innovation." A breakdown of this study yields the following significant findings: immigrant-owned firms have a higher propensity to conduct all types of product and process innovation as well as research and development activity, and immigrants have a higher propensity to develop goods or services that no other firm offers. While these studies are not specifically tailored to small businesses, the assumption that similar findings exist across the board for all sizes of business is logical. Furthermore, because the vast majority of immigrant businesses are below fifty full-time employees just by their nature, this data can be accepted as applicable for the purposes of our research.

All of the aforementioned findings provide scientific backing to an otherwise intuitive thought process about immigrant-owned firms. Personally, when I think of immigrants, thoughts of their courage and determination come to mind. I have always admired that these people have put tremendous effort into a sophisticated immigration process, knowing that they would face even more hardships upon arrival. I will continue to respect immigrants for the sacrifices they made to build better lives for themselves and their families. With these beliefs held close to the heart, I often found myself approaching research expecting immigrants to outperform native-born citizens in the spheres of business because they have more to lose and hardly anything to fall back on should a venture fail.

A research paper seeking to identify the success strategies of immigrant small business owners included a phenomenological study based on interviews with these owners. Using a conceptual framework based upon cultural theory, five themes emerged among owners of small businesses that were deemed "successful," where success was defined as surviving beyond five years. These themes were "strong work ethic and family dynamics, flexibility and independence, limited societal barriers, business experience, persistence, and great customer service." These may not seem to be novel findings, but backing these socially-supported ideas with research is valuable when evaluating and creating policy. Further, cultural theory (which extends cultural belief and value at the national level indicates that immigrants "have cultural traits such as hard work, strong communal ties, frugality, and risk acceptance" (Buechel, Hellmann, & Pichler, 2014) (BHP). This finding has significance when looked at in tandem with the research that states that "immigrants can see advantages and opportunities through a cultural prism when they arrive in the country, and their motivations, as well as emotions, have a cultural component" (González Rey, 2014) (BHP). Research from a wide range of studies has commented on the contribution of inherent cultural values to post-immigration success in their new nation. Kourtit & Nijkamp in 2012 concluded that the strong social values of immigrants enhance dedication and support business. Wennberg et al. in 2013 found that "fear of failure in business ownership has a link to culture" (BHP).

There is a particular value of highly educated immigrants to the United States economy (IAI). A. Mushfiq Mobarak, an associate professor of economics at the Yale School of Management, identified how immigrants have contributed to the United States economy as top developers of innovative products and scientific findings. On the Organization for Economic Cooperation and Development tests, which are administered to secondary school students to measure aptitude in mathematics and science, the United States consistently ranks near the bottom relative to other developed nations. Yet, the United States has persisted in being the home of immense talent and innovative companies, and it possesses a comparative advantage in both science and innovation. Mobarak credits this anomaly to the existence of universities in the United States capable of supporting and fostering such innovation, which attracts highly-educated immigrants. Along with his colleagues, he has published findings that indicate "increases in the supply of foreign students subsequently result in significantly greater publications and citations from science and engineering departments in the United States" (IAI). Born in Bangladesh, Mubarak acknowledges the potential for a "win-win" situation when the United States attracts talented foreign-born people and gives them the opportunity to interact with the innovative universities and companies present here.

Partnership for a New American Economy put out a large report explaining how immigrants are driving small business creation, and therefore economic growth, in the United States. Using the data from the American Community Survey, the Current Population Survey and the Survey of Business Owners, the report indicates a strong connection between immigration and job growth. The central points focus on the likelihood of immigrants to start businesses relative to their native-born peers, the increase in immigrant entrepreneurship despite a "lagging" economy, and immigrant-related job creation and exports. Over the last 15 years, immigrants have increased in likelihood to start a new business while native-born Americans have become less likely too. Immigrants are more than twice as likely to start a business as native-born citizens—with a business formation rate of 550 new businesses per month per every 100,000 immigrants relative to only 270 new businesses per month for every 100,000 native-born citizens. As of 2011, immigrants were overrepresented in this regard; they make up 12.9 percent of the population, but start 28 percent of new businesses (NAED).

The investment in immigrant entrepreneurs is far greater than their current value, especially since the demographic has indicated trends of growth among the group even in slower economic times. In 1996, immigrants composed only 15 percent of new business owners. A mere decade-and-a-half later in 2011, immigrants started 28 percent of all new U.S. businesses. While the start-up rate of immigrants has nearly doubled, the rate of U.S. natives starting new businesses has declined by about 10 percent over the same fifteen-year period. This census data makes it clear that the country is increasingly reliant on immigrant entrepreneurs to drive new business growth. Immigrants indisputably contribute to the economy. Immigrant-founded startup companies comprise 51% of those that are worth over $1 billion dollars in the United States as of 2015, according to the National Foundation for American Policy brief (NFAP). In 2007, immigrant-owned businesses employed about 4 million workers and paid nearly $127 billion in payroll, a statistic/demographic that has continued to grow (IFO).

Furthermore, industry-specific findings also suggest that immigrant entrepreneurs will have a growing responsibility in keeping the United States economy afloat. In seven of the eight sectors that the U.S. government expects to grow the fastest over the next decade, immigrants start more than 25 percent of businesses. The industries—health care and social assistance, professional and business services, construction, retail trade, leisure and hospitality, educational services, transportation and utilities, and "other services"—all have an outsized share of businesses founded by immigrants. In these industries, immigrant-owned businesses are thriving. In 2010, they generated over $775 billion in sales. Of this $775 billion in sales, $100 million was income—more than 20 percent of all income generated in the aforementioned sectors.

Immigrant-owned businesses do not just drive certain industries; they drive the entire effort of the United States economy in areas such as exports. The importance of exports has been argued by the CATO Institute to be an indicator of the state of the economy as a whole and an indicator of job growth. This is based on research that found in 22 of 25 years from 1983 to 2007, GDP, trade, and job creation increased and decreased in unison. More intuitively, increasing exports helps creates domestic jobs by shifting the trade imbalance a bit more in favor of the United States. The statistics continue to support immigrant-owned business as a large driver of overall exports. The NAE report states that immigrant-owned businesses are about 60 percent more likely to export compared to native-owned businesses. This high percentage is at least in part attributed to the pre-established networks in their home countries, a greater understanding of local markets and needs, and shared language and culture that minimizes trade barriers. Finally, immigrant-owned businesses are over two-and-a-half times more likely to export more than 20 percent of their sales than native-owned businesses. The efficiency of allowing immigrant entrepreneurs to fill a niche in which they can use their culture and business expertise to create stronger companies in the United States is evident.

Many previous research reports have solely focused on the contributions of highly educated immigrants. While attracting these immigrants is important and certainly offers economic and social value, the data indicates that immigrants of all education levels are finding success by creating businesses after immigration. Statistics indicate that more than 37 percent of new immigrant business owners lack a high school diploma, compared to 16.4 percent of native-born citizens. Looking at the micro-level, communities that attract people of lower education levels are often those which are the most economically and socially distressed. Given the affinity of immigrants to start small businesses, they have the potential to stimulate economic activity in some of these communities by increasing the number of job opportunities and in turn combatting high unemployment rates.

Many immigrant small business owners are aware of the concept of "paying it forward." Practically no one successfully can start and grow a business from the ground up without the goodwill and help of at least one other person. This generosity does not hit a dead-end when passed on to immigrant entrepreneurs; it is recycled and passed on as the immigrant business owners gain traction within their industries. Dr. Abe Dalu of A&A Reliable Home Health Services is a member of the Oromo Chamber of Commerce, which supports other motivated workforce members of his ethnic group. Kateri Guitterez of Collective Avenue Coffee runs an internship program to provide working opportunities to inner-city youth within a five-mile radius of the coffee shop. These interns started off as mostly high school students in the summer of 2018, but the program expanded to include college students and recent graduates. As a substitute teacher in her hometown where the coffee shop is located, Guitterez is well-oriented within the community to attract students who can most benefit. By allowing interns to participate based on how much they want to contribute to projects, such as updating the media kit and cafe's website, Kateri provides structured volunteering that prevents exploitation of their unpaid labor and time. Both Dalu and Guitterez exhibit a selfless dedication to supporting the development of their peers and mentees to help position them for their own future success. Additionally, both of these immigrants operate businesses rooted in giving back to their communities—providing care to the disabled and elderly and serving as an open forum for productive conversation, respectively.

CHAPTER 5

ROSIE PAULSEN ENTERPRISES

Rosie Paulsen is the epitome of the American Dream. The founder of three successful businesses, she has grown to be a widely respected figure by her home community of Tampa Bay. Rosie has lived in the United States for over 30 years. Her parents, both teachers working full- and part-time jobs, were unable to make ends meet in their native Ecuador. This, complemented by Rosie's persistence to come to the U.S. since her first visit at age 12 (as Rosie put it, "Either we go now, or we go now!"), lead to their family's fragmented move stateside. She left Ecuador at the age of 18 along with her sister to come to the United States. After a few years, her dad successfully moved to Tampa, Florida. Over the course of a few more years, her brother and mother came to the U.S., eventually allowing for their family to be reunited and put down new roots in Florida. "And then, life happened with me."

One need not look far to see that Rosie is an established businesswoman and citizen. She is a woman who wears many hats. As described on her LinkedIn: "As a speaker, she specializes in educational seminars on Medicare, the Hispanic market, and entrepreneurship. As a civic leader, Rosie believes in economic growth through collaboration and forming long-lasting relationships. As a talk-show host, Rosie highlights local business owners, their involvement in the community, and how they inspire their paying customers to do business with them" (LINRP). Additionally, as Commissioner of the Florida Commission on the Status of Women, she works to promote communication and collaboration among all organizations focused on the welfare of women in Florida. In her capacity as commissioner, she is a central resource for lawmakers and businesses seeking education on the issues that affect women, girls, and their families. In each of these positions, Rosie adheres to her brand of "Pure Positivity" centered upon restoring society through "inspiration, determination, and my Pure Positive attitude."

Where Rosie's story is particularly fascinating is the variability between her work experiences and how she has built upon each experience to create a product better than the last. Her earliest job in the U.S. was working for American Express as a customer service representative serving various business people. In 2004, she started working with health care provider Humana Healthcare, where she had her first taste of her future passion: Medicare. Despite her lack of experience selling anything and lack of an insurance policy to call her own, she began helping retirees get Medicare insurance plans. Directly servicing the Hispanic community was not her initial target market, yet the opportunity arose when she was the only Spanish-speaking representative employed at her office. She filled a niche by serving the Hispanic community of the Tampa Bay area, which enabled her later business ventures and social entrepreneurship. At some point during these years, Rosie also founded a Hispanic Chamber of Commerce in hopes of further improving her community. While it is no longer in existence as of 2014, it served as an important learning curve for Rosie. She then took the concept of the chamber and used it as the central focus of her enterprise, Rosie Paulsen Enterprises.

With her first taste of success and entrepreneurial nature, Rosie decided to go independent instead of working for Humana Healthcare. In 2009, she founded her first company, Good Faith Insurance Services (GFIS). GFIS was a brokerage firm for Medicare, enabling her to sell a wider variety of plans than she was able to as an agent at Humana. In turn, she found she was able to provide customers with a more personalized product. This satisfied an initial source of discontent at Humana—Rosie never wanted to sell someone a plan that was not right for them just because that was what her employer offered. As many small business owners have shared, Rosie says the hardest part of her job was getting in the door as an entrepreneur. In an industry so reliant upon trust and the customer experience, Rosie's personality and prior knowledge became the backbone of her business. Rosie explained her GFIS operations as being a "matchmaker for health care." As a broker, she matched people with policies that they then stay "married" to for the rest of their lives. Operationally, Rosie reviews her clients' policies annually to ensure she is still servicing them as best she can.

Setting out on her own and starting GFIS was an unlikely path for Rosie. As the daughter of two teachers, she was not educated in the language of insurance and residual income—but she overcame these family obstacles and found success. Being an entrepreneur was a taboo in her family; "my parents are uncomfortable with entrepreneurship because you never know where your next dollar is going to come from." As with many immigrants who come to the United States on a quest for financial stability, the looming possibility for failure by entering the uncharted territories of founding a small business was daunting to her at first. It was Rosie's personal determination that ultimately led to the foundation of GFIS. "I realized that the American Dream is owning your own companies, so you don't have to be dependent on a nine-to-five job." So, after staying within her comfort zone for about four years to learn more about insurance and the basics of entrepreneurship, she started GFIS. "When I did it, I never looked back."

In the time since Rosie first became a small business owner, the changes she has observed have been both positive and tangible. Rosie recounted that upon entering the insurance industry, there were very few females, and those few female agents "were older and white, and the industry as a whole was dominated by older Caucasian gentlemen." Aside from demographics, Rosie also identified a shift in mentality. Her early competitors were those who grew up in a cut-throat training environment, while Rosie has stayed true to her personal belief that selling insurance "is not about killing people over a policy, it is about building a meaningful relationship." She was able to take her previous experience at American Express, which was primarily about providing stellar customer service, and apply it to the health care industry when she opened her brokerage firm. Pairing prioritization of the customer experience, her knowledge of Medicare, and the value of relationship-building became central to Rosie's business strategy. This is how she achieved the "winning product" for her agency. With this strong foundation, she then set about creating a brand and marketing strategy. Rosie is a business owner capable of finding synergies between the various overlaps in her professional life. Using her leadership position as the head of the Hispanic Chamber of Commerce, she helped the aging population by being a clear touch point for Medicare information and services. Identifying this customer segment and focusing on Medicare in the Hispanic market enabled the growth of GFIS.

Rosie did not stop there. Following the success of GFIS, Rosie set about expanding to create a second company. With her female business partner, Rosie co-founded Good Faith Company and Casualty (GFCC). This company diversified from just offering Medicare to offer other insurance products instead, such as life and property insurance. GFCC soon experienced the same rapid growth as GFIS. Rosie took the agency from being merely a concept to a carefully crafted brand employing ten insurance agents. In line with her mission of promoting the growth and collaboration of Hispanic entrepreneurs, she eventually sold the company to two of her employees. Rosie is a firm believer that each agent can do better if they are their own agents. This freed Rosie up to pursue her next lead while still maintaining a modest flow of income from GFCC to help support herself and her future ventures.

This next pivot married Rosie's professional experience and passion for being more than just as an insurance broker. "These businesses have been great ideas, but how can I help other segments of the population?" In the city of Tampa, 98% of the economy is driven by small business owners. In the larger Tampa Bay area, 78% of the economy is driven by small businesses. The composition of the economy of Tampa has created what Rosie identifies as "highly reliant on the relationships you've built despite the big-city feel." These statistics, coupled with her ideology that society as a whole benefits when small businesses are thriving, led to the formation of Rosie Paulsen Enterprises (RPE).

The old adage, "third time's the charm," held true in Rosie's case. RPE was the culmination of her knowledge from her previous two businesses and a marriage between her entrepreneurial skills and professional expertise. The central goal of RPE was to teach people how to be successful in business. Its conception dates to Rosie's experiences at the Hispanic Chamber of Commerce. Many struggling small business owners who are seeking guidance and aid are unable to leave their offices and stores. It is, in turn, extremely difficult to get advice and a flow of paying customers coming into their stores. Specific to the service industry, it is hard for business owners to showcase themselves and what they do. This oversight, Rosie realized, was in part due to a lack of online visibility. Rosie's shift of focus to social media as a valuable tool in growing a business was integral to RPE's success. After realizing the importance of social media in growing companies, she took a course dedicated to Social Media in Business. Rosie took the class and got her certification to "prove herself, and everyone else, wrong" about the unimportance of social media. "I know how to build relationships and how to help guide people through business exchanges." With her new knowledge of social media, Rosie realized that starting her new company would provide people with the opportunity to learn from her acquired knowledge and strengthen their own business skills.

The day-to-day operations of RPE split into two branches. The primary branch features workshops for small business owners that focus on identifying their purpose and finding the right steps to grow their business. Rosie's ideology is that "no one else can do what you were created to do." She further explains, "A lot of people do not know their purpose. Be it life purpose or business purpose. When you can identify the synergy between the two, you are heading in the right direction. If you fail to do so, you are being led in two different directions." Rosie has taken it upon herself to help her workshop attendees on the journey of finding their purpose. After this, she walks them through a carefully constructed structure to convey this and put forth their best, most well-rounded self. With their newly identified business purpose, she then shifts their focus to working on the business. They do this through smaller, tangible activities such as creating goals for brand image, a 30-second infomercial, and outlining the target market. In tandem with the deliverables, Rosie also holds networking events for workshop attendees. Each event consists of twenty to twenty-five people and is held early in the morning so that all the business owners can run their respective businesses during the traditional workday. This interesting business model is a prime example of an immigrant using the knowledge and resources at their disposal to propagate the success of the community as a whole.

The other, arguably more fun and dynamic, branch is "Where's Rosie?" This is a segment of her website where Rosie shares updates about her day.

With her popularity in Tampa, many look to Rosie as a navigator of various networking and community events. Her judgment to identify valuable events is trusted by her business-owner peers. While the feature started as a joke, within two months of its introduction, Rosie found that people started coming to events to see her, saying, "We found Rosie!" "Where's Rosie" is a nod to the power of social media in connecting business owners and expanding personal networks.

RPE is continuously growing thanks to Rosie's constant willingness to experiment with new ideas. For those unable to attend her workshops, her guidance is available remotely. "Cafecito with Rosie," which directly translates to "small cup of coffee with Rosie," is a show where Rosie shares her advice and knowledge. The show is featured on local TV, YouTube, and on some Hispanic radio stations. As a bilingual immigrant, Rosie is always conscious of the language in which she delivers her information. Her Hispanic descent has influenced her professional focus to cater to the Hispanic community. While Rosie's workshops are in English, she records radio segments in Spanish. Starting in 2019, Rosie began taping the shows in English and in Spanish for TV and posting them on YouTube. (You can find Cafecito on Rosie's YouTube Channel, Rosie Paulsen Enterprises).

As from her businesses, Rosie continues to actively contribute to her community. For people who need Medicare information, she hosts Medicare 101 presentations. By pairing up with local doctors, she is able to reach a larger audience of senior citizens in need. Rosie increases the transparency of the Medicare acquisition process by helping people learn the basics. Acknowledging the confusion surrounding Medicare, especially for other immigrants who are not literate in American health insurance vocabulary, is the start towards getting these people effective care. She comes equipped with explanatory materials and distributes them to presentation attendees. Rosie welcomes discussion and questions, even doing follow-up talks to meet the patients' needs. These presentations are done in Spanish, although Rosie hopes to expand to do bilingual presentations by the end of 2019.

Rosie has identified that in response to the language barriers, many Florida doctors are learning of the importance of knowing Spanish in the medical field. The need for presentations of this nature has drastically increased in recent years as the tail-end baby-boomers are turning 65.

Specifically, 16.7% of Tampa Bay's population was above the age of 65 as of 2016, according to the Tampa Bay Times (TBT). This same article identified Tampa as one of the oldest metro areas. With earlier intervention, these older individuals are more inclined to make educated Medicare decisions, which have positive outcomes for the remainder of their lives.

As we touched upon earlier, the demographics of the industry have changed. Rosie now estimates that 45-50% of the meetings and conferences she attends for Medicare agents are young Hispanic women. On the small scale, Rosie likes to think that she has not only found her passion for entrepreneurship but has inspired other women to claim their seats at the table and take control of their professional destinies. "I went from being the only person in the room to a member of the majority."

The medical insurance industry is far from isolated. Many trends that Rosie has identified in her businesses hold true for a variety of other businesses across her county and, in some cases, the entire nation. One such policy that Rosie observed in her community was that some companies began doing training programs for how to sell Medicare policies exclusively in Spanish in 2018. This is a point of contention, one on which Rosie has a distinctive opinion. Rosie worries for two reasons about only training employees in their native language of Spanish. First, she is concerned that this will put workers at risk should they lose their job, as not learning English puts them at a tremendous disadvantage in the U.S. job market. The other aspect is that Rosie believes that all U.S. residents should be able to speak decent English. "If you are selling something, you need to speak English. The problem is that the demand is so great among Hispanics that these brokers do not feel the need to diversify and sell to English-speakers." An example of this would be an insurance broker in Puerto Rico who immigrates to Florida but does not speak English fluently. It is easier for the Florida agency to help them get a certification in Florida than it is to expend the resources necessary to find, educate, and train a new broker. This essentially says, "Don't worry about learning English now because we need you to get right to work." Rosie believes that this perpetuates a cycle in which it is difficult for these people to then contribute to society and support themselves beyond catering to the Hispanic community.

In conversation, Rosie referred to herself as the poster child for why the ACA fails business owners. Prior to the ACA, Rosie and her husband held a medical insurance policy at a private insurance company where they paid about $150 a month in addition to deductibles. This was in addition to a $10,000 catastrophic policy, which also had monthly payments of about $40. With the introduction of the ACA, their medical insurance increased up to $450. Even with the $100 subsidy, they still were paying $350 monthly. The following year, their policy increased to a whopping $650. The Paulsens were paying $500 more monthly for the same policy. At this difficult intersection, they questioned the value and sustainability of their present insurance plans. Rosie and her husband decided it would be easier and more affordable to instead pay the penalty, which was part of the Individual Mandate. "I was the person selling you insurance without having an insurance policy for me and my husband because we cannot afford one." Rosie attributes this legislative oversight to the identified brackets. For those who fall within the annually set ACA brackets, the Act is beneficial. But, for those who fall above or below, affording health insurance is a huge challenge. Despite this obstacle, Rosie has succeeded as a businesswomen.

With each new business venture, Medicare presentation, and conversation, Rosie hopes to give a voice to her community. This voice is important in the political arena as well. She believes that the tendency of her community to be silent when it comes to discussions about politics has led to a misunderstanding of their true beliefs. "We are so indoctrinated by the media that we created the idea that we are little people, standing beside big people. That we are little people without thinking, speaking, or acting in their own interests." Because of this, she tries to empower small business owners with her knowledge. Rosie wants to be the one who gives people the awakening. She is on a personal quest to help Hispanic people understand and differentiate between their true beliefs and what others tell them they are. She gives advice to them and alternatives to being indoctrinated as they presently are. Rosie hopes to amplify the political focus on the needs of small business owners by using her own voice. The lessons that Rosie teachers her SBOs span beyond just work advice; she also teaches immigrants how to embody the American Dream by empowering them to vocalize their beliefs and enact change that benefits themselves and their communities. Once they successfully do this, they are able to build and improve successful businesses within these communities.

Aside from ethnic stereotypes, Rosie acknowledges the importance of business owners finding their voice and actively participating in politics. "Although politics might not be at the center of the discussion in my community, I realize that as someone living in the United States, I have to get involved. My vote does count, and I am responsible for that one vote." Rosie's political goal is to educate people to think outside the box—and beyond the black and white lines on the ballot. Regardless of political party, "I just care that people are thinking for themselves without other people planting ideas in their head," Rosie says. Especially as an immigrant, Rosie believes that people want to make you think that your vote does not have an impact, that it won't make a difference. Yet, she has come to learn that in this country, it does make a difference. She compels all business owners to live with the mentality that "I have to do my research and believe that this one vote will make a change." Rosie says, "if you own a business and are not comfortable talking about politics, then you are at a disadvantage because your business, at one point, can get hurt by you not getting involved in the government." An example of this was in Hillsborough County, Florida, close to Rosie's home district. The public of Hillsborough voted in support of increasing a tax to 9.5% when it was placed on the ballot. Rosie believed people were swayed by its presentation on the ballot, which focused on benefits that would accrue thirty years from the time of the vote. The difficulty is that now people are driving (in some cases up to 40 minutes) outside of the county to do their shopping in order to avoid the tax. Unfortunately, the business owners of Hillsborough are, in turn, struggling. Rosie wonders why the chamber of commerce was not advocating for the small business owners that they're supposed to be serving about this tax. Further, she identified a deficiency in the education of the public on the implications of the tax. "If the 98% of the county composed of small business owners and dependent citizens is going to get hurt with this tax, why was there a lack of advocacy against it?" Rosie believes it is the civic responsibility of citizens to educate themselves when lawmakers do not support their best interests, and she urges the Hispanic communities of Florida to do just that. In an effort to practice what she preaches, she has served on steering committees and gotten involved with communicating to the government her fellow citizens' needs.

Immigrant small business owners are a community amongst themselves. Within this community are a constant flow of stories and a built-in support system for shared obstacles. Rosie shared with me the story of a good friend of hers (who will be referred to as Sarah for purposes of anonymity). Sarah came to the U.S. from Venezuela with an E2 Investor Visa. When her visa expired, it was not renewed. By the time Rosie learned about her friend's un-renewed visa, Sarah had already sold her company and moved back to Venezuela with her two children. The tragedy reached deeper than just her professional life. While in the U.S., Sarah married a Mexican man whom she was forced to divorce due to his inability to return to Venezuela with her. Rosie shared that, in addition to these difficulties, the children spent a lot of time inside the house because of all of the violence near their home in Venezuela.

While she was unable to help Sarah, Rosie has found a way to make this terrible story a learning situation. She now gets involved in her friends' immigration processes by asking what type of visa they have, and if they have E2 visas, she has them check their expiration dates. "It's terrible that I had to see my friend go through this before realizing the importance to be better educated about the U.S. visa process."

Access to financial capital is another huge obstacle Rosie acknowledged for immigrant small business owners. Part of the difficulty is the variation between local banks and how they are regulated. Every bank has its own unique legal requirements, which means that no two banks guarantee the same loan outcome, rates, etc. Especially in the case of smaller, local banks, relationships with owners and managers can be instrumental in getting loans. Rosie shared that in her personal experience, she was able to get a loan more easily due to a professional relationship with an employee of the bank. Rosie stresses the importance of having a specific loan strategy and the inter-reliance of various loans. For example, even if you get an 85% loan from the FBA, you may need to get 50% from the local community. Without the proper approach, the loan recipient is back to square one and is hindered from making financial progress.

Rosie is the common denominator of success for many of her workshop attendees. "I see them grow, when they're little, when they're big, and the connecting factor is that they all know Rosie! I know it's the passion and drive to help people." During the Obama Administration, she was invited to the White House for an economic prosperity meeting for local small business owners of the Tampa Bay area. At the meeting, they discussed how they can help unify business owners and the government to overcome the present challenges. In her more immediate community, she has met with local senators. "Once I get to the right people that are able to make improvements, I can use my knowledge, experience, and patience to help people achieve a better way of doing things." She has been invited to roundtable discussions to talk about how to best allocate resources for the community and shared her thoughts with her senators. Rosie has succeeded in using her platform as a businesswoman to make herself an advocate for immigrants in her community.

CHAPTER 6

ETHNIC ENCLAVES

When I first learned about ethnic enclaves (geographical concentrations of an ethnic group) in my world history class in high school, the concept made sense (CORE). As humans, we are attracted to a sense of comfort which is inherent to people who are most similar to us. it is logical that people with shared ethnicities and therefore languages and cultures would cooperate to attain a larger, shared success through establishing a unified front with their countrymen. I was wrong, however, in the locations I had pictured this happening. I pictured the various ethnic ghettos where people had emigrated from the same country two or three generations ago. I pictured minimal interaction outside of said communities—a self-sufficient group of people completely in touch with their ethnic roots.

I pictured Astoria, New York, as my grandparents (Yiayia and Papou, as I call them) had described it to me: bustling sidewalks full of people shouting in Greek beneath the inevitable roar of the Long Island Railroad with its 15-minute intervals. I see my Papou Steve, working as a furrier in the basement of a brick building I walk outside of today, hunched over a sewing machine as it hums quietly into the late hours of the evening. As I sit in my church and listen to the service delivered in Greek, I feel the same sense of camaraderie that my grandparents felt; a sense of unity beyond just language and tradition, one that consoles the buried emotions from leaving behind the familiar village and embarking on the treacherous journey across the sea to an unknown country. I was wrong not only in my superficial thinking that the isolation of such groups would be willfully maintained, but also in my failure to grasp the greater economic implications these communities could have on the United States as a whole.

Ethnic enclaves are related to immigrant-owned businesses beyond just the high tendency of immigrants to be self-employed compared to native-born citizens. Ethnic entrepreneurship is an academic field of study that focuses on the processes immigrants follow to become entrepreneurs (SPRIN). For many, settling within ethnic enclaves represent the first stepping stone towards a comfortable adjustment and later success as entrepreneurs. Additionally, for many immigrant entrepreneurs, the enclave is an integral part of their "social and cultural context," especially as a location where access to ethnic resources can be found. It is within the ethnic enclave that social networks can be harnessed for both employees and customers (ARC). Study after study has found that immigrants outpace native-born Americans in starting up new businesses and dominate their competitors on the entrepreneurial activity index. Toussaint-Comeau found that immigrant-owned businesses have a tendency to be clustered in distinct neighborhoods, in which their owners often obtained the resources to start said business. Her study also explored whether the ethnic enclaves and their related networks influence the decision by immigrants to become self-employed. Findings have indicated that despite patterns in geographical concentration and self-employment rates, it ultimately depends on which ethnic group is being discussed. For example, Cubans have both high geographical concentration as well as above-average rates of self-employment among immigrants in the U.S. Contrarily, immigrants from India are more dispersed upon immigration, yet they still have above-average rates of self-employment. And yet, despite the success of Cubans and Indians regardless of geographic concentration, Mexican immigrants are extremely concentrated geographically yet they are relatively underrepresented in businesses. These three examples begin to show that there is much more to the value of ethnic enclaves beyond just concentration of an ethnic group. There are a variety of factors that go into the enclaves' influence on entrepreneurship: 'quality' of the social or business network, job market factors, and other personal characteristics.

As is recognized in the different rates of self-employment between Cuban and Mexican immigrants, the quality of the social and business networks inherent to the enclave is an important consideration. Generally, ethnic enclaves have become known as particularly good locations for the formation and maintenance of such networks. This is due to their nature of being "cohesive social units" (which derives from sharing a common language, culture, and religion). As enclaves are immigrant communities with many newcomers, they possess a concentrated group of people with similar "timing," in that they all have difficulty obtaining information on business, housing, schooling, and other information. Acknowledging the stifled access to such information is when the social and business networks grow to satisfy those particular needs. These networks serve ethnic enclave members as sources of information and connection to other immigrants from their ethnic group (CORE).

Ethnic enclaves have not only persisted into the twenty-first century, but thrived in creating self-sufficient markets for certain goods and bustling economies. More specifically, in some instances, ethnic enclaves succeed in providing goods and services to consumers for lower prices than multinational corporations are able to achieve. Due to globalization and the large movements of workers across regions in search of employment, there is a growing demand for small businesses in urban areas. These businesses are capable of tailoring to their particular ethnic audience in a more price efficient manner than a large company, which may not be able to hone in on products particular to a certain ethnic group. Additionally, global restructuring of labor markets has created changes on the local level, including an increased number of immigrant or ethnic minority businesses (as found by Strüder in 2003).

The flexible business activities that these small businesses are capable of—such as altering product offerings to better suit a particular ethnicity of customers—keep them apace (or ahead) of rapid economic change. Through supporting ethnic enclaves, the nation is, in a way, arranging insurance for future crises. This can be accomplished by allowing for the spread of new ideas and the attainment of new opportunities in current climates (SPRIN).

Conceptually, arguments stand on either side for whether or not ethnic enclaves have positive labor market outcomes (IFNSE). As mentioned above, the positive attributes center around the social benefits of participation in a residential neighborhood where ethnic and cultural backgrounds are shared. The enclave is a prime setting for immigrant entrepreneurs to satisfy the demand for "ethnic goods" which appeal strongly to a particular group

(CORE). Membership in a social network has positive peer-effects such as access to information about job opportunities or knowledge of the job application process. While these do not directly relate to entrepreneurship, it is success within the enclave's firms and communication among residents that opens the door to new small businesses and allows pre-existing ones to thrive. On the other hand, there are inherent obstacles for immigrant entrepreneurs who settle in enclaves. Self-employment may be a less viable option in economically poor enclaves due to residents lacking purchasing power and thereby limiting the potential for business growth (CORE). Physically, there is difficulty acquiring the skills—such as proficiency in the native language—which are vital to successful integration into the native labor market. On more profound levels, ethnic enclaves have been shown to produce "an economic stranglehold" by preventing immigrant interaction with external alternatives beyond their immediate community. Further, it has been found that while living in enclaves, there may be facilitation of social and institutional "distance" from natives due to perceived self-sufficiency within the enclave itself. Without a consensus among researchers, we can turn to specific instances where enclaves have had a clear effect on market outcomes.

The above observation that smaller immigrant-owned businesses are able to succeed despite turmoil in the rest of the economy has been repeatedly identified. One such example was in 2008, when Dr. Alethea Hsu successfully opened up a new shopping center that was nearly fully leased despite the widespread financial turmoil occurring across the country. Hsu, a Taiwan native, opened the retail complex in Irvine, California, with her Diamond Development Group. With no context, it is shocking that Hsu would succeed in this venture while industry giants, such as General Growth Properties, were struggling to avoid bankruptcy. Yet Hsu credited her success to an understanding of ethnic markets relative to the general population. In an interview, she explained that her mostly Asian customers—the Korean, Chinese, Taiwanese, and Japanese residents in Orange County—were a demographic who still had cash on hand, both in savings and as money to spend. For Hsu, it came down to understanding the core ethnic values rather than following financial news reports. She used her knowledge about the population that would bring business into the stores leasing at her property and adapted her small business accordingly. Hsu has further explained that regardless of where

Asians are—be it in California or in their homelands—they tend to be "big savers." As a result, they have the cash to buy goods despite down-turned markets and contradictory behaviors of other customers. There is a growing divergence, as shown by Hsu, between ethnic markets and those that appeal to the general public as a whole. As in Hsu's case, appealing to a well-understood segment of the population (particularly a certain ethnic group contained within a geographic region) has the potential to expand despite mainstream centers suffering or failing at the same time (FORBES).

However, this research does not guarantee enhanced entrepreneurial success in enclaves as opposed to pursuing business from a wider range of clients. A number of studies focusing on how conditions in immigrant enclaves of metropolitan areas affect entrepreneurs have indicated that Mexican immigrants experience less success than small business owners of other ethnicities, such as Koreatown in Los Angeles. Therefore, we can reach the intermediate conclusion that the existence of a firm in an ethnic enclave has an indeterminate influence on the success of the business.

That being said, the promises of ethnic enclaves to the entire United States economy should not be overlooked. Some immigrants arrive searching for a sense of familiarity in the United States that will enable them to "get on their feet" and help them lay the foundation necessary for success. Some find their footing with the help of previously immigrated family members or with an American citizen with whom they have been communicated. Yet, for a portion of people who come largely independently, ethnic enclaves provide a connection to their country of origin that they might otherwise lose. For this reason, ethnic enclaves are a place where migrants and diasporans (INDERS) can nurture their distinct characteristics of entrepreneurship. These enclaves provide important resources and networks that must precede the discovery of business opportunities.

A paper by Elo et al. focuses on the Finnish diaspora in Oregon to understand how transnational diaspora entrepreneurship has evolved over time. The Journal of International Management defined transnational diasporan entrepreneurs as "migrants and their descendants who establish entrepreneurial activities that span the national business environments of their countries of origin and countries of residence" (SDC). The Finnish case study found that as generations integrated into life as diasporans, the dissolution of their Finnishness (and Finnish identity) in regards to entrepreneurial activities influenced the recognition of opportunities. In other words, the transformation of their social identity had tangible effects on their entrepreneurial spirit and success.

The scale tips both ways, however, when it comes to analyzing how acculturation influences future entrepreneurial success. It has come to be accepted that fostering immigrant entrepreneurship plays a large role in creating a stronger economy. This has been shown to be true in various case studies of particular cities, but understanding the factors that influence the immigrants' decision to engage in entrepreneurial activities must be at the base of the discussion. For instance, Ruiz et al. touches upon the above assumptions of enclave effect on labor markets; they found that acculturation is negatively related to business ownership over the past decade among recent Mexican immigrants in the U.S. (RUIZ). Acculturation is the assimilation of immigrants to a different culture, typically the dominant culture of the country to which they have immigrated. As such, when the Mexican immigrants further dissociated from their Mexican culture—an outcome which was measured by identifying how the cultural context influenced opportunity recognition among laborers—they gained access to a wider range of information about job opportunities. In turn, the exposure to such information promoted economic mobility and entrepreneurial attitudes in the long run. Additionally, it was identified that within the social networks inherent to the enclave, immigrants were able to obtain the informal training, learning, and skill acquisition necessary to succeed in the jobs about which they received information from each other. These Mexican enclaves demonstrated the value of specialized social networks to accumulate resources for the creation of more jobs (Masurel et al., 2002; Ruiz et al., 2017).(MASU AND RUIZ)

Similar research was conducted on Chinese immigrants. Like other immigrant entrepreneurs, the Chinese have been observed to have the tendency to start up small businesses within their ethnic enclaves. A study in 2010 illustrated that Chinese immigrant entrepreneurs succeeded in using ethnic network resources to minimize transaction costs and thus enhance business performance and increase profits. Using such networks for business and other information gives a comparative advantage to members of the ethnic enclave relative to native business owners. This same research found that there is negative effective growth outside of the enclave community due to the exclusive reliance on strong ties within the enclave. It was also concluded that the more transnational entrepreneurs relied upon ethnic embedded resources and network structure, compared to societal resources shared by the whole public, the less likely they were to expand the scope of their business beyond the enclave's direct needs and demands (ARC).

All of the above research on ethnic enclaves has social and political implications in addition to the economic implications. The contained nature of ethnic enclaves can lead to negative perceptions of immigrants and negative attitudes towards immigration as a whole. There is a perceived threat that the asylum provided by enclaves isolates immigrants from social integration and assimilation to native cultures. As a result, there is an overall lack of social cohesion and a myriad of government programs aimed at achieving unity. The presence of ethnic enclaves is not black and white, but a vast gray area to policymakers. Beyond consideration for various ethnic groups and respect for their cultures and traditions, the potentially drastic economic effects (both positive and negative) wrought by the enclaves must be accounted for (ARC).

The effects of living in an ethnic enclave on immigrants' labor market outcomes have received significant attention in previous research (Edin et al., 2003; Damm, 2009; Portes and Zhou, 1993). Whether and how ethnic enclaves influence various labor market outcomes for their residents is a scientific inquiry with important policy implications. For example, knowledge of how the residential location of immigrants is linked to their labor market integration can aid the development of refugee placement programs, labor market integration policies, as well as city planning. Consequently, such effects are widely debated among policymakers and politicians in most western countries.

Ethnic enclaves play a tremendous role in facilitating immigrant business performance and social integration. (ARC) The existing research on the variability in outcomes dependent on the ethnicity discussed, location, concentration, and a number of any factors shows the lack of a definitive conclusion to be made about ethnic enclaves. In the larger discussion of immigrant entrepreneurship, these enclaves are an important structure to consider as contributors to their success or failure dependent on the case.

CHAPTER 7

COLLECTIVE AVENUE COFFEE

The Affordable Care Act (ACA), like all of the health care legislation that preceded it, has had tremendous effects on the daily operations of businesses. In particular, small businesses have had to respond and adapt to the ACA mandates. Each small business owner rises to the challenge differently when confronted with the difficulties wrought by the ACA. One of such small business owners is Kateri Gutierrez of Lynwood, California.

Kateri Gutierrez is the daughter of Mexican immigrants. She was raised in the Los Angeles area, where immigrants make up a significant portion of the population. Kateri's internal drive led her to start her own business, and her proximity to a thriving immigrant community was extremely influential to the decisions which laid the foundation for her business. While born in the United States, Kateri's awareness of the contributions of immigrants instilled in her the importance of supporting and enhancing her community. After attending the University of California, Berkeley, and working as a substitute teacher, Kateri set about creating a worker cooperative, or worker co-op. Worker co-ops are working environments where everyone contributes to the common good of the company rather than reporting to a single boss. They are a place where employees not only work but also enjoy the profits of the business. Just as her upbringing was supported by a unified community, her business endeavor would also be structured as people coming together to experience shared success.

Among business structures, a worker cooperative is not entirely similar to the more traditional small business compositions such as sole proprietorships, partnerships, or limited liability companies. Worker co-ops are democratically-run-and-owned businesses. The United States Federation of Worker Cooperatives (USFWC) provides the following definition:

> "Worker cooperatives are values-driven businesses that put worker and community benefit at the core of their purpose. In contrast to traditional companies, worker-members at worker cooperatives participate in the profits, oversight, and often management of the enterprise using democratic practices. The model has proven to be an effective tool for creating and maintaining sustainable, dignified jobs; generating wealth; improving the quality of life of workers; and promoting community and local economic development, particularly for people who lack access to business ownership or sustainable work options" (WOCOP).

Within a legal framework, cooperatives have various corporate forms depending on the state, yet all co-ops must consist of mechanisms through which workers make decisions that affect the performance and governance of the business. The USFWC states that the majority of cooperatives are small businesses in the retail and service sectors, but there is also a developing presence of cooperatives in food production, sales, technology, and home care.

In order to join the USFWC, which is the predominant federation uniting worker cooperatives in the United States, the businesses must adhere to the following seven principles:

1. Voluntary and Open Membership
2. Democratic Member Control
3. Member Economic Participation
4. Autonomy and Independence
5. Education, Training, and Information
6. Cooperation among Cooperatives
7. Concern for Community

Joining the USFWC offers a range of benefits to member worker co-ops, including Kateri Gutierrez's business, Collective Avenue Coffee. It is a prime example of a business rooted in these principles. When talking about her own co-op structure, Kateri is proud to say there is no boss at the top of the pyramid or outside investors whose voices dominate decision-making; it is purely worker-run. In order to have a say in the operations or future of the business, you have to take an active role due to this unique composition. Co-ops offer a wide range of benefits, such as improved treatment and wages of workers, democratic participation for the betterment of a larger group, creation of long-term stable jobs, and development of linkages across the social economy. Worker cooperatives do more than just provide their employees with a place to work; they teach their members skills and values that are important in today's democratic society. By virtue of working at Collective Avenue Coffee, every worker develops the ability to engage with their community. They take these skills with them beyond the workplace to local government, school organizations, and nonprofits.

After completing her due diligence in researching business structures, Kateri ultimately decided upon creating a worker co-op. She next set upon thoughtfully deciding what type of business to introduce to her community. After careful consideration, she chose to create a coffee shop for several reasons, the primary being the atmosphere of the shops. Kateri sees the value in the ambiance of a coffee shop—a space that encourages conversation, provides a space to think, introduces you to your fellow coffee-drinker, and creates a community. Kateri shared that she admires the "ripple effect of conversations at coffee shops" and jumped at the opportunity to propagate such a productive outcome in her own community. She then found and subsequently decided upon collaborating with her now-business partner Jonathan Robles, a trustworthy confidant with the experience in the specialty coffee industry and the business expertise necessary to transform drafts of her business plan into a reality. The two business partners "envisioned a shop that would bring specialty coffee and artistic spaces" to their hometown of Lynwood, California. With these ideas, beliefs, and strong values, they set about creating Collective Avenue Coffee as a coffee shop capable of affecting positive change and contributing to Lynwood's economic progress.

As so many small business owners quickly discover, operating a business is much more than the original ideas of macchiatos and mochaccino.

Responding to the calling of entrepreneurship is a unique experience—where thought, effort, and excitement surrounding the business idea are accompanied by many unforeseen logistical operating details. Kateri was now responsible for issues relating to insurance, safety, risk management, and health care. By empowering herself as a small business owner, she took the responsibility to find sufficient health care not only for herself, but also for her future loyal employees. In conversation, she explained to me the health care transition from being a public school substitute teacher to a small business owner. As a substitute teacher, she had no health coverage from her employer. As a result, she had to depend on the government for insurance in order to avoid paying the financially overwhelming Individual Mandate levied upon those who do not have approved health insurance plans (SBM). Kateri expressed that the individual mandate fee was a "big financial burden" and lamented that if she "was not financially literate, she would have struggled even more." After transitioning to becoming a small business owner, Kateri found herself in a very similar state. She once again had to acquaint herself with an unfamiliar landscape of health care demands. She was no longer in the realm of coffee but had inserted herself into risk pools, deductible plans, and health reimbursement accounts.

The fact that a Berkeley-educated college graduate struggled to navigate through the intricacies of the basic U.S. health coverage system indicates a dire problem. If formally educated members of society are having difficulty understanding how to properly face a universal government fee, this only highlights the weaknesses inherent in the American health care structure. Kateri further shared that she felt "lucky as a millennial" when she acknowledged that if she had been from a generation that was less tech-savvy, approaching this health care minefield would have been even more daunting and complex. Additionally, she took a personal finance class in college that aided her ability to manage multiple financial accounts simultaneously, a skill she doubts she would have had without this component of her education. How well business owners are equipped to advocate for their health care interests is instrumental in determining the quality and cost-effectiveness of their health care insurance plan options. Kateri's situation was unique in that she herself was already getting health insurance elsewhere.

With her previous intimate knowledge of the complexities and impediments of health care acquisition, Kateri left her job as a substitute teacher, partially due to the mounting costs and complexities and frustration of securing her own health care coverage. When I spoke to Kateri, she was receiving health care from the nonprofit she simultaneously works at rather than through Collective Avenue Coffee. Kateri is no stranger to the fact that health coverage has enormous implications on workers' decisions to work for a certain employer. Armed with her comprehension of the necessity to acquire health care, she has attempted to use her understanding of the complexities and impediments of health care acquisition to improve the working environment for her employees. So, while Collective Avenue Coffee does not offer complete health care plans to its employees due to size and cost implications, Kateri does strive to provide what she can for her fellow cooperative-workers. She does so through membership of the aforementioned USFWC.

Collective Avenue is one of 200 businesses that are members of the USFWC. These members include workplaces ranging from worker cooperatives and other democratic workplaces to cooperative developers and allied organizations. To join, the cooperatives must apply using a membership application and then subsequently meet with the membership director to confirm eligibility and determine the member class of the business. To maintain membership and receive "benefits," businesses must pay annual dues (which are calculated in a formula dependent on member class).

The USFWC has a mission of "building health equity and mobilizing our membership to create better, more affordable options for health care." It accomplishes this by providing resources and benefits to members. Specifically, the USFWC currently offers dental and vision benefits and is in the process of piloting general health insurance coverage in certain states. In the future, USFWC plans to sponsor retirement plans and offer reduced rates on business insurance. While California is not one of the states with general health insurance coverage, Collective Avenue Coffee workers do receive their dental and vision care through the USFWC benefit providers.

As the majority of worker cooperatives are small businesses, those involved in the USFWC are no stranger to the difficulty inherent in obtaining health care. The introductory documents to the plan themselves explain that the USFWC health-related benefits plan was developed because it's "too hard for cooperatives to get good dental and vision plans that don't have hidden terms and surprise costs." With this mentality, the USFWC aims to provide a plan that is easy to use, affordable, and transparent with admin fees that are kept as low as possible.

The logistics of the USFWC health-related benefits are very clearly disclosed both on their website and in the hour-long informational webinar provided on their website. The dental rates are provided through Ameritas, an employee benefits and financial services company, while the vision rates are provided through EyeMed (the associated vision plan offered by Ameritas). The breakdown of costs includes monthly administrative rates per organization, and the premium rates vary depending on enrollment type deductibles and annual maximums. The administrative rates cover the cost that USFWC incurs by running the program—which is essentially a convenience and improved accessibility fee for the cooperative itself. Administrative rates depend on the size of the business; the smallest and cheapest group for 1-10 employees, the next for 11-25 employees, and the largest and most expensive for 26+ employees. Premium rates increase based on the enrollment type—either single, employee & child(ren), couple, or family (in that order).

Another unique aspect of the USFWC health-related benefit offerings is the call for employers to provide the maximum amount of health care for their employees. Despite not being a governmental organization, the USFWC recognizes the positive community benefits associated when workers have to pay less for their health care plans. Consequently, the USFWC encourages workplaces to pay workers' monthly health-benefit premiums in their entirety and go so far as to require the workplace's minimum payment of 50% of its workers' monthly premium in order to remain eligible to participate in the offered benefit plans. This requirement, while straining member businesses that might not have the profit margin available to have large health care expenditures, is invaluable for supporting the financial interests of the worker and the business in the long term. Additionally, this speaks to the larger values of worker cooperatives and how workplaces can continue to hold themselves to a higher moral standard.

The USFWC is a prime example of how the unification of a larger group comprised of smaller like-minded groups can create for the most efficient route towards affordable health resources. Data from the most recent annual census estimated that across the United States there are more than 500 democratic workplaces, employing over 8,000 people and generating about $400 million in annual revenues (USFWCO). As more and more businesses become USFWC members and utilize health-related benefits, Ameritas and EyeMed become more incentivized to maintain the plan. In turn, the administration costs are streamlined for each small business by USFWC and the premiums and rates are lower than they would have been across the board had these same small business approached providers on their own. Additionally, the plans purchased as a larger group through the USFWC possess more widespread access to care than many of the smaller plans accessible to small businesses on their own.

CHAPTER 8

CURRENT POLITICAL CLIMATE

When it comes to discussions of immigrant small business owners, public policy is at the heart of the discussion. How the government approaches immigrant entrepreneurship is rooted in the public opinion of immigrants as much as it is rooted in solid research, which showcases their success in contributing to the greater national economic stability. Focusing this chapter on policy discussions revolving around the subject group of immigrant small business owners sets the scope of related policy to encompass a much more specific repertoire of legislation.

Immigration policy is a fascinating topic in itself, with many intricacies worthy of discussion. Even more fascinating, and perhaps troubling, have been the hasty changes made to decades-old policies since the inauguration of President Donald J. Trump in 2016. These changes have not been devoid of their share of nationwide outrage and protests, which have not only modified public opinion but established immigration policy as worthy of attention on the political agenda. The purpose of this writing is in no way to share political beliefs but to adopt the perspective of the immigrant population—saturated with self-employed small business owners—as these legislative changes have influenced their livelihoods, families, and journey towards becoming United States citizens.

The Immigration and Naturalization Act (INA) is the body of law that governs immigration policy, setting the limit for the number of permanent immigrants and per-country numerical ceilings. Meanwhile, aside from the INA, the United States admits temporary noncitizens and the legislative and executive branches annually determine the number of refugee admissions. Lawful permanent residency is outlined in the INA as allowing a foreign national to live and work permanently in the United States, regardless of employment status. There are several key principles that serve as the basis for immigration law: "The reunification of families, admitting immigrants with skills that are valuable to the U.S. economy, protecting refugees, and promoting diversity" (AIC). Following these principles are the policy subcategories of family-based immigration (which focuses on family unification using a sponsor system consisting of Lawful Permanent Residents and U.S. citizens), employment-based immigration (which grants temporary visa classifications), and an annual quota of permanent employment-based immigrants. Additionally, there is a Diversity Visa Program and an affiliated lottery system that focuses on allowing immigrants from countries with low rates of immigration to the United States to secure green cards. Fragmented from the above immigration law are the policies granting legal admission to protect refugees, those seeking asylum, and other vulnerable populations. These policies are on the basis that the above groups are fleeing from persecution or are unable to return to their homeland due to extraordinary or life-threatening circumstances. Subsequent to entering the country as a Lawful Permanent Resident—or a dependent of one as determined by familial association—a person must maintain LBR status (green card) for a minimum of five years in order to qualify for U.S. citizenship through naturalization. Applicants are then required to be at least 18 years old, demonstrate continuous residency, pass exams (in English, U.S. History, and civics), demonstrate "good moral character," and pay an application fee, among other requirements. By the time many of these immigrants have jumped through all the hoops to obtain U.S. citizenship, starting a business may not seem all that difficult (AIC).

Even before the changes brought by the Trump Administration, obtaining citizenship in the U.S. was a difficult and lengthy process. Title 8 on Aliens and Nationality of the U.S. Code of Federal Regulations (8 U.S.C. § 1601) (GPO) states that "self-sufficiency has been a basic principle of United States immigration law since this country's earliest immigration statutes" (USCIS). While self-sufficiency is often one of the goals immigrants attain in the later stages of cultivating successful small businesses, it is hardly what we first observe when they arrive in the United States. Many of the small business owners I have spoken to have shared stories of working one—and oftentimes multiple—jobs in areas that did not best utilize their expertise as a way of establishing a footing in their new country. In the early stages of their citizenship, they need a bit of help, but in the long run, these are the same people who are creating jobs and contributing to the greater national economy. When it comes to discussions of immigrant small business owners, the related policy includes a much wider scope due to their nature of belonging to a few select groups who are often the focus of American lawmakers. They are classified with the immigrants themselves but also in the various laws aimed directly at regulating or supporting small businesses as a subset of the United States' economy.

One particular change is the impact of newly designed "Public Charge" classifications to immigrants who are seeking permanent residency while living on visas (Allen). Historically, the classification of being "liable to become a public charge" was utilized by immigration officials to evaluate the amount of reliance new immigrants had on the government as a criterion for their candidacy for permanent residency in the United States. In the past, the "public charge" group included immigrants receiving Supplemental Security Income and those living in long-term nursing home care facilities supported by the government. The revisions to the rule would greatly expand the criteria for which immigrants are deemed to be of Public Charge. Under the new definition, people who utilize Medicaid, Medicare Part D, public housing, and the Supplemental Nutrition Assistance Program (SNAP) would all be deemed to be liable to become a public charge and therefore denied admission to permanent residency (i.e., receiving a green card) on those grounds. Essentially, larger numbers of legal immigrants would be prevented from transitioning to become permanent residents and full-fledged citizens.

There are tremendous complexities that accompany any change in the wording of a rule which affects such a large group of people—specifically, the U.S. Citizenship and Immigration Services Office states that 91% of all adults in the labor force would be impacted by this change (USCIS). The range of the programs included—such as aid in finding suitable housing and access to nutrition and health care—further magnifies the impact wrought by the change. This is especially true in the case of small businesses that are not yet large enough or do not generate enough profits to provide health insurance to their employees. This change could potentially force employees to decide between paying for food and health care for their families versus candidacy to become permanent American residents. Another consideration is that households are the units to which the classification would apply, causing whole households—with mixed groups of citizens and noncitizens—to disenroll from the newly included programs. Further, the analysis of the costs and potential benefits of this change succeed in not only conveying its gravity but also in expressing the risks. Looking at the total annual income of workers who might leave the United States as a result of the change suggests a negative indirect economic effect of about $68 billion dollars (Grounds). Additionally, there are the less-quantifiable changes, such as the destabilization of certain industries if the Public Charge change pushes them to move underground. Particularly, the construction, mining, natural resources, recreation, and food services industries are all volatile due to the large percentage of noncitizen workers who would be affected by the law change (Grounds). The entire situation becomes even more complex when it is considered that undocumented workers pay billions in taxes each year—often primarily through the Individual Tax on their earnings—subsidizing the aforementioned programs regardless of their status or ability (and lack thereof) to enjoy them. A country whose arms were supposedly open to those in need is now encouraging those same people to willfully give up the benefits that their income tax pays for.

The difficulty in expanding the definition of Public Charge is that the research supporting its expansion does not even begin to include the stories of immigrants who received these non-cash public benefits and currently give back to society with as much—if not more than—the amount they received from the government initially. It is a change that seems to say that "income and wealth determine one's value to society" (NYTO). One such immigrant is Kam Tam. As he told the New York Times, he had active tuberculosis when he emigrated from China at the age of sixteen, weighed a mere 96 pounds, and had a dental catastrophe in his mouth. Upon his arrival, he received care at a publicly-funded community health center, which got his health back on track. Free of tuberculosis and rotten teeth, he pursued his education in the U.S. by attending both college and pharmacy school. Today, as a businessman and pharmacist, Dr. Tam generously donates both services and financial resources to needy families in Oakland. Dr. Tam is just one of many success stories that would not have been written in the first place had the recent rules passed earlier. The situation of Public Charge is just one amidst a wider scope of anti-immigrant legislation, drawing pushback from many cities in which immigrant groups and sympathizers have united to express how essential immigrants are to strong economies. Immigration protests took place nationwide on June 30th, 2018, in cities including Los Angeles, New York, and Washington D.C. (CNNC), with passionate chants such as "sin papeles, sin miedo" (translating to "no papers, no fear") and the support of celebrities.

In addition to making it harder for people to get green cards, Trump has also made other efforts to terminate programs that support immigration (NPR). Two such programs are the Temporary Protected Status program, which he attempted to end, and Deferred Action for Childhood Arrivals (DACA), which he did end. The Temporary Protected Status (TPS) "is a temporary immigration status provided to nationals of certain countries experiencing problems that place their nationals at risk if deported there or that would compromise the foreign government's ability to absorb the return of its nationals" (AICRT). The reasons why a country may be designated for TPS include ongoing armed conflicts, environmental disasters, and other extraordinary and temporary conditions. While a judge blocked Trump's efforts to end the program (VOXI), its threatened existence serves as a reminder of the uncertain future for immigrants in the United States.

While judicial resistance succeeded in upholding TPS, DACA was not as fortunate. DACA allowed individuals brought to the United States as children or teens before 2007 to apply for protection from deportation and work permits as long as they met certain requirements (such as enrollment in high school or college, no criminal convictions, and being under the age of 16 when they entered the country). The program did not provide these children with lawful immigration status but instead granted a deferral from being removed from the U.S. and work permits to those who qualified and successfully renewed their membership every two years. At the end of 2017, the Trump administration formally announced it would end the Obama-era DACA program. DACA granted legal protections to about 800,000 people who entered the country illegally as children. Ending the program has enormous implications on the lives of the self-proclaimed "DREAMers" (DACA recipients) as well as preventing people from applying for enrollment in the program moving forward. While valid permits remain in effect until they expire—except in instances of termination or revocation—there will be tremendous uncertainty when the two-year permits are up. For many DREAMers who were brought as children with their parents, the threats of deportation back to their country of birth is unfathomable, especially because they might not remember living in such countries and have adjusted themselves to life in the United States (NPRO). With the change in administrations from Obama to Trump and the entirely different approaches to immigration policy, it is difficult for immigrants to wholeheartedly contribute to the United States economy and ignore the constant threats to their residence status.

These changes brought about by the Trump administration reach further than just counteracting President Obama's changes; they also call into question how immigration policy affects the national economy. In fact, it goes all the way back to Abraham Lincoln. Lincoln recognized that "immigrants are one of the replenishing streams appointed by providence to repair the ravages of internal war and its waste of national strength and health" (VOXP). During a time of the toxic white supremacy during the Civil War, Lincoln signed "An Act to Encourage Immigration" into law. Allowing immigration is not purely an act of charity, but, as Lincoln understood, a strategy to strengthen the United States. The viewpoint that having a larger and more diverse population supports a more complex division of labor and more efficient development of resources explains how immigrants ultimately contribute to a more sophisticated and successful national economy. In these scenarios, looking at the bigger picture is always extremely valuable. Equally valuable is logically applying analyses, such as cost-benefit analysis, to societal decisions. A University of Chicago Booth School survey of well-known academic economists found that a majority agreed admitting more "low-skilled immigrants to the United States would make the average U.S. citizen better off" and all 89 panel-members agreed more highly-skilled immigrants would be good (BOOTH).

Beyond political obstacles, immigrants face other barriers put in place by society that increase the difficulty of starting their own business.

Rohit Arora, an immigrant entrepreneur from India, said that "despite small businesses being among banking institutions' most profitable loan clients, many entrepreneurs and small business owners from South Asia and India seem to be having trouble securing bank loans, even though such entrepreneurs boasted low default rates" (RNAE).

Small business owners are a testament to the potential within each citizen to ultimately better their own lives and the lives of those around them. Having this heightened awareness of how even the most minuscule changes in policy can alter individual lives (and eventually entire industries) is invaluable in policy analysis. Conversations about local politics are an integral part of moving policy in a direction that supports rather than constricts the expansion and success of small businesses. Furthermore, the mobilization of citizens in supporting small businesses through being conscientious of the laws which potentially restrict their owners is critical to laying a foundation for productive future generations to continue to develop successful businesses from the roots up.

Despite the obstacles that have been erected with the changes in immigration policy, there have also been tremendous and thoughtful efforts to help immigrants on both the local and national levels. Nationally, under President Obama, the White House launched the Startup America initiative in 2011. An aim of the Startup America initiative was to create the right policy environment for "entrepreneurs to flourish" (OWHA). At the presentation of the initiative, Obama was quoted saying:

> "Entrepreneurs embody the promise of America: the idea that if you have a good idea and are willing to work hard and see it through, you can succeed in this country. And in fulfilling this promise, entrepreneurs also play a critical role in expanding our economy and creating jobs." (OWH)

While Startup America was not solely directed towards immigrant entrepreneurs, portions of its focus certainly supported their success. In the same vein, the Department of Homeland Security announced a variety of initiatives to reduce barriers and "make the government work" for immigrant entrepreneurs. Using new waiver programs, visa types, and streamlining the visa process, Obama sought to attract foreign entrepreneurs by providing visas for those looking to start businesses and helping promising foreign graduate students in STEM stay in the country after graduation.

Another large aspect of Startup America was achieved when the Department of Homeland Security clarified that the eligibility of immigrant entrepreneurs for existing visa categories had been increased for science, technology, engineering, and math (STEM) graduates, who were able to extend their work training in the U.S. The efforts of the Obama White House were not lost; in fact, there have been various success stories of immigrants who credit Startup America for increasing the ease for immigrants to create businesses in the U.S. One of such immigrants is Manu Kumar, an immigrant to the United States at the age of 17 in 1992 from India (OWHA). Since his graduation from Carnegie Mellon University, he has helped found four companies—three of which have been acquired. His first business, a software company known as SneakerLabs, which he began while still attending university, was sold for over $100 million and consisted entirely of U.S. citizen employees. As an investor, he has helped fund 15 companies. Collectively, he has been involved with companies that have created over 400 jobs in the United States. One of such changes from the Startup America initiative which expands the number of graduates who can stay in the U.S. for 17 additional months on top of the 12 months after graduation granted to foreign students through the Optical Practical Training program directly impacts immigrants like Kumar in the present day. As a serial entrepreneur, he is candid about how immigration policy has impacted his trajectory: "I can also see that there were several points along the journey where I almost failed—not because of lack of ability or effort, but because of a system that presented challenges for an immigrant entrepreneur to stay in the United States." Since receiving his green card under the "Alien of Extraordinary Ability" category, he has continued to embrace his entrepreneurial spirit. Kumar is vocal regarding the potential he sees for immigrants, like himself, to thrive and thereby improve the United States workforce. "I strongly believe that the best thing the United States can do to attract and retain the smartest people from all over the world is to encourage these people to start their companies right here." It is with these beliefs that Kumar commended the American government for "making efforts to realize the full potential of our existing immigration laws to attract the best and brightest from around the world."

There have also been many successful immigrant business initiatives aimed at particular cities and immigrant groups. The New American Economy 2019 Mid-Year Report shared the importance of proper integration of immigrants into society:

> "Immigrant entrepreneurs and immigrant workers of all skill levels want to reside in places that welcome them. Thus creating an all-inclusive environment becomes a key to attracting businesses that are vital to economic development. With the support of both civic and business leaders, working to welcome immigrants contributes to economic growth, global competitiveness, and local diversity. Some cities are already seeing the economic benefits of immigrant-friendly policies" (AACO).

Rather than waiting for cues from Washington to initiate policies, many cities have begun to introduce their own policies to encourage a culture of inclusion and opportunity for all community members, especially immigrants. Generally, the policies focus on undertaking initiatives that make government services more easily accessible to newcomers, streamlining immigrant access to employment in certain industries, promoting programs that celebrate diversity, and encouraging participation in collaborative community projects. By increasing interaction between immigrants and locals, cities such as New York City and San Francisco have found that trust is built between natives and immigrants. Below are a few handpicked examples of how immigrant entrepreneurs have been supported for their contributions to the economy across the United States (HBSFP).

Competition THRIVE Program: New York City

Immigrant entrepreneurs own more than a third of New York City's 200,000 small businesses. In order to celebrate and support both the creative and economic ecosystems of these immigrant entrepreneurs, the city introduced its annual Competition To Help Reach Immigrant Ventures and Entrepreneurs, commonly identified using the acronym THRIVE. According to the program website, the competition "encourages new and innovative ideas that assist immigrant entrepreneurs in starting, operating, and expanding their businesses in New York City." Competition THRIVE invites organizations to develop proposals focused on promoting growth opportunities for New York City's immigrant-entrepreneurial community. Winning plans enable immigrant entrepreneurs to start, operate, and grow their businesses in New York City. The competition is structured so that five finalists receive $25,000 to put towards piloting their program. After the pilot period ends, the most successful program receives an additional $100,000 for continued program implementation. Success during the pilot period is judged accordingly to the proposed plan, and criteria include everything from revenue generated from licensing fees to behavior changes.

Finalist projects of Competition THRIVE support immigrant entrepreneurs using a range of strategies. Each finalist is selected based on utility, sustainability, and scalability of the proposed project. The Business Outreach Center (BOC) Network supports construction businesses owned by immigrants by forming a support system that would allow for combined training and networking activities. A more technical approach was taken by the National Community Reinvestment Coalition (NCRC), a project which consists of a web application where immigrant entrepreneurs can address difficulty accessing capital and formulating local business connections, two integral components in growing a business. With five finalists selected each year to introduce their projects, New York City is taking the initiative to equip immigrant businesses with the tools necessary for success (NYEDC). The finalists behind the BOC Network explained that "cultural competency and knowing when to change outreach strategy is essential" when it comes to making programs accessible to the targeting immigrant community. Another finalist, the Queens Economic Development Corporation, shared that "success is not only about having business acumen, but being able to develop human relationships with program participants." As these two quotes have shown, it is beneficial to shift the narrative towards including immigrants as another group able to contribute to society (NYEY).

International Institute of St. Louis: St. Louis, Missouri

The International Institute's website describes it as a "welcoming center for new Americans" with a mission statement of helping "immigrants and their families become productive Americans and champion ethnic diversity as a cultural and economic strength." The Institute services over 7,500 immigrants and refugees from 80 countries each year. Economic development is a major goal of the institute, and it is achieved through providing business and asset development services, such help constructing a custom "Development Plan" with a Business & Asset Development Specialist, which covers managing cash flow, the legal side of starting a business, and accounting. Betsy Heller Cohen of the St. Louis Mosaic Project said, "Particularly in a region like ours, when we have less than the national unemployment and workforce issues, making sure that we find ways to both welcome foreign-born people and use their skills to fill our economy is a priority" (NSTLP).

Welcome Dayton Plan: Dayton, Ohio

The Welcome Dayton Plan is an initiative focused on the integration of immigrant-friendly policies and practices within the city. Originally introduced in order to reinvigorate the declining population in the post-industrial Rust Belt metropolis, they plan itself contains policies including English-language classes and multicultural soccer tournaments. Additionally, it called for the creation of a community-wide campaign dedicated to immigrant entrepreneurship to rejuvenate the global markets of Dayton. A study by the U.S. Chamber of Commerce Foundation found that the efforts included in the Welcome Dayton Plan succeeded in strategically creating a more welcoming culture and attracting immigrants to the city.

The Office of New Americans: Chicago, Illinois

In 2011, Mayor Rahm Emanuel declared that he would make Chicago the most immigrant-friendly in the world. A testament to his vow, he created Chicago's Office of New Americans that has partnered with an advisory committee and philanthropic organizations to create a set of initiatives called the New Americans Plan, which includes strategies for welcoming immigrants and maximizing their contributions to Chicago upon arrival.

Welcoming Cities Initiatives: Across the Nation

The organization Welcoming America launched an initiative known as "Welcoming Cities and Counties" that "offers local governments the opportunity to commit publicly to advancing a welcoming culture and policy agenda" (AACO). Since its introduction, 25 municipal governments representing a population of over 24 million have been joined by civic and business partners in promoting a welcoming atmosphere to immigrants.

Programs that support the transition for transnationals helps all Americans—both immigrant and native-born—to build stronger economic and social ties. Furthermore, even those programs and policies which are not directly focused on promoting small-businesses development have made significant contributions to small business entrepreneurship by providing immigrants the tools necessary to become established as active community participants with the connections necessary for entrepreneurial success.

CHAPTER 9

INTERNATIONAL ENTREPRENEUR RULES

The conversation about what policies the United States government creates regarding international policy holds extreme importance to how immigrants currently in the United States live. From setting the parameters in which their businesses function to determining how they live their everyday lives, legislation has a tremendous effect on immigrants in our society. These policies will continue to dictate the success of immigrants as entrepreneurs. More specifically, rules pertaining directly to international entrepreneurs can serve as opportunities, or conversely, barriers to those considering coming to the United States (USCIS).

The International Entrepreneur Rule (IE Rule) was initially published by the Department of Homeland Security (DHS) under the Obama Administration on January 17, 2017. The rule contained a unique strategy for boosting economic activity in the United States: revise regulatory processes and criteria for foreign entrepreneurs to be paroled into the country. Under the IE Rule, the parole authority of DHS is given more flexibility. They are able to use this authority to evaluate and grant periods of authorized stay to foreign entrepreneurs on a case-by-case basis. The foreign entrepreneurs would be eligible for the authorized stay if they succeeded in demonstrating that their stay in the United States would "provide a significant public benefit through their business venture and that they merit a favorable exercise of discretion." The IE Rule specifically relates to small businesses because it specifically stated that parole would be granted to entrepreneurs working for their start-up business.

The eligibility criteria outlined by the DHS is as follows (USHH):

- Possess a substantial ownership interest in a start-up entity created within the past five years in the United States that has substantial potential for rapid growth and job creation.
- Have a central and active role in the start-up entity such that they are well-positioned to substantially assist with the growth and success of the business.
- Will provide a significant public benefit to the United States based on their role as an entrepreneur of the start-up entity by showing that:
  o The start-up entity has received a significant investment of capital from certain qualified U.S. investors with established records of successful investments;
  o The start-up entity has received significant awards or grants for economic development, research and development, or job creation (or other types of grants or awards typically given to start-up entities) from federal, state, or local government entities that regularly provide such awards or grants to start-up entities; or
  o They partially meet either or both of the previous two requirements and provide additional reliable and compelling evidence of the start-up entity's substantial potential for rapid growth and job creation.
- Otherwise, merit a favorable exercise of discretion.

Each of these criteria encourages immigrant entrepreneurship as a route to stay in the United States.

In July of 2018, the DHS delayed the effective date of the rule to March of 2018 so that its consistency with President Trump's Border Security and Immigration Enforcement Improvements Executive Order could be checked. The Executive Order directly states that the executive branch hoped to "end the abuse of parole and asylum provisions currently used to prevent the lawful removal of removable aliens." Despite making enormous strides with support from certain academic and political circles, in May 2018 (USHH) the Department of Homeland Security proposed to eliminate the IE Final Rule. An update on the U.S. Citizenship and Immigration Services Website cited that the elimination was because the department believes that the rule "represents an overly broad interpretation of parole authority, lacks sufficient protections for U.S. workers and investors." The DHS itself cited that upon review it planned to propose the removal of the IE Final Rule because "it is not the appropriate vehicle for attracting and retaining international entrepreneurs and does not adequately protect U.S. investors and U.S. workers" (USHH). Even though the IE Final Rule will be eliminated, it still provides for an interesting conversation about international entrepreneurs and gives a view into the government's stance on immigration in the current policy climate (USHH).

With the election of President Trump in 2016, it became evident that job creation was a nationwide concern. Segments of the population were attracted to the notion that Trump promised his administration would bring jobs back to the American public, especially by combatting offshore job sourcing. As described in an article by Bloomberg, the Trump immigration policy is based on the core principles of upholding the law of the land and promoting a "merit-based" system to help the economy (BERG). With both of these goals in mind, the case-by-case analysis of immigrant start-up creators the DHS had initially proposed seems in line. The economic benefit of attracting top entrepreneurs to create their startup companies in the United States rather than elsewhere— where they would contribute to the already fierce global competition our nation faces—is clear. This same Bloomberg article cites that it would have created approximately 300,000 jobs in the United States and that the original eligibility criteria rule out 99.99996% of the population. These two statistics alone advocate for the exclusivity of the merit-based nature of the rule and the tremendous potential for economic development.

CHAPTER 10

ROLE OF NONPROFITS AND ONLINE RESOURCES

Without immigrants, there are no immigrant small business owners. Yet, the politics surrounding immigration are difficult to ignore. With such a polarizing issue, it is not difficult for political beliefs to overpower research on actual immigrant contributions. After all, the winning presidential campaign slogan in the 2016 election was to "Make America Great Again," which in part insinuated that immigration had tarnished America's shine. As immigration has persisted in holding its spot near the top of the political agenda, citizens must to shift their glance a bit to the side—to look at the various non-profit organizations sharing valuable information and organizing enormous efforts despite anti-immigration reforms. The success of these non-profits is a manifestation of the value of social change and taking an interest in the civic, social, and economic concerns. The following organizations have had magnificent impacts on the public opinion of immigration and, in many cases, have had a direct influence on the communities in which immigrant small business owners have begun their businesses. Their impacts go to show that legislation need not be a be-all-end-all and that active citizens can work to educate society on topics they believe in.

A Partnership for a New American Economy: (NAEW)

A self-proclaimed "bipartisan research and advocacy organization fighting for smart federal, state, and local immigration policies that help grow our economy and create jobs for all Americans," NAE has been making waves in immigration reform circles since its creation in 2017. Launched by New York City Mayor Michael Bloomberg and media mogul Rupert Murdoch, NAE strives to bring policymakers and the public closer to comprehensive immigration reform. Upon its conception, Bloomberg explained, "NAE will enable Mayors and CEOs to demonstrate to policymakers the vital role that immigration plays in our economy by publishing studies, conducting polls, convening forums, and sponsoring public education campaigns" (WIKI). NAE advocates for immigration in three ways: use of powerful research to demonstrate the impact of immigration on the American economy, organizing grassroots and influencers to build support for immigration, and partnering with state and local leaders to support policies that recognize the value of immigrants.

The first of these strategies revolves around using data and narratives from immigrants to shine a positive light on immigration. From the very beginning of NAE's research efforts, they found that 40 percent of Fortune 500 companies were founded by immigrants or their children. It is findings like this that showcase how immigrants are thriving in entrepreneurship and working to build prosperity across the United States. Additionally, NAE has many research-based articles that measure the value of immigrant contributions to specific industries, such as their role in the $100 billion national agriculture industry. NAE research isn't confined to industry divisions; it also provides quantitative immigrant contributions on a geographical level. Research from NAE and other similar organizations is an integral part of the conversation about the important role immigrants play in the economy and the greater society.

The next strategy aims to influence those on either side of the political spectrum by equipping them with the necessary information and means to make the economic case for immigration. NAE has led coalition-building efforts with immigrant leaders, religious leaders, business leaders, and grassroots leaders. NAE has worked with organizers in more than 100 districts across 33 states in an effort to get the ears of members of Congress.

In 2017, the NAE collaborated with the American Action Forum to publish a pro-immigration open letter containing their research-based core economic arguments. (The letter was signed by 1,470 economists.) In tandem with the local approaches of the NAE, there have also been tangible instances in which NAE intervention has represented the best interests of immigrants. As the Trump administration moved toward rescinding DACA, NAE launched their iMarch campaign. Through iMarch, they utilized supporters and stories from every congressional district to highlight flaws in the current immigration system and sought potential solutions for DREAMers. Moving mountains is no easy task, but with NAE carefully constructed base, iMarch's coalition-led effort was extremely well-received. The effort was featured on more than 100 media outlets, had on-the-ground events in every state, a central hub in the U.S. Capitol Building and a reach to approximately 4.5 million people on social media.

The third and final pillar of NAE is to focus on local immigrant contributions so that communities can feel and acknowledge their value. The NAE State and Local Team works to promote policies and programs centered on creating jobs and facilitating economic development. Currently, there are NAE State and Local Teams active in more than 50 communities, over 80% of which are in conservative states. By focusing on the state and local political landscapes, NAE has succeeded in making more tangible short-term changes, such as strategic plans for immigrant integration and the introduction of state Seals of Biliteracy. NAE has also partnered with Welcoming America to create the "Gateways for Growth Challenge" which enables local governments, nonprofits, and chambers of commerce to jointly apply for "tailored research, direct technical assistance, and matching grants to support their strategic planning process" (NAE). NAE has also worked alongside chambers of commerce across the nation to create the "Global Talent Chamber Network" to connect these groups.

Throughout this writing of this book, NAE articles and reports have been invaluable. Not only are they extremely helpful, they are clearly conscious of the role of immigrants on the local level and have done a tremendous job highlighting those immigrants who have thrived as small business owners. For these reasons, I nod to NAE as a central source for pro-immigration economic information and commend them as a powerful group of advocates grappling with the complex American reception of immigrants to our nation.

Welcoming America

Unlike the research-based and economy-focused approach of NAE, Welcoming America is an on-the-ground movement supporting immigration across the country. Welcoming America "leads a movement of inclusive communities becoming more prosperous by making everyone feel like they belong." Built on the belief that the success of every community (and of our shared future) is dependent on the contributions of all people, including immigrants, Welcoming America has drawn the roadmap and provided the support necessary for all residents to be welcomed to their communities. Welcoming America offers two large "asks" for participants: joining their various networks and participating in their annual Welcoming Week.

Launched in 2009, Welcoming America has had monumental success across the United States. As a non-profit and non-partisan organization, Welcoming America has worked to foster a culture and policy environment that invites newcomers to fully participate in their new homes. Currently, their social entrepreneurship model has been used to strengthen communities by encouraging the participation of all people in economic, civic, and social life. The efforts of WA cannot be boiled down to a single program or service, but rather consists of unique local approaches to enable each community to take the necessary steps towards reducing barriers that prevent full participation of immigrants.

The aforementioned social entrepreneurship model includes three central approaches. First, Welcoming America connects leaders in the community, government, and nonprofit sectors to their far-reaching network for support and guidance. Second, they build upon existing community efforts by providing tested methods and approaches known to benefit creating a welcoming environment for immigrants. Third, they enact change through helping communities draft policy, reinforce welcoming principles, and understand the socioeconomic benefits of promoting inclusion. Using this generalized approach, Welcoming America has established a presence in a wide range of communities and has synthesized successful strategies to achieve its mission.

While much of Welcoming America's work may initially seem abstract, they truly are making tangible changes. There are various programs that allow nonprofit and government partners to engage in transforming their own communities. For example, the Welcoming Network membership program "offers tools, resources, technical assistance and global network" in which participating members have access to coaching strategy sessions with experts, educational services, and peer-learning based community exchange programs. Welcoming America has also created the One Region Initiative (ORI) focused in the metro Atlanta area consisting of a comprehensive plan to make the region more welcoming to immigrants. The pillars of the plan include civic engagement, government leadership, safe communities, connected communities, equitable access, economic development, and education. The plan itself is to be implemented by a regional development by a Steering Committee composed of political figures, community members, nonprofit directors, and business executives. By introducing the plan towards creating a more inclusive region, Atlanta expects to see increased economic development and leverage for business attraction, in-depth resident investment "as evidenced by business entrepreneurship, school enrollment, and community engagement," and an improved status as an innovative leader amongst a nationally competitive economic environment (WAON).

For areas not directly engaged in a plan like metro Atlanta, Welcoming America still has opportunities for involvement. Every year, Welcoming America holds a national Welcoming Week that consists of a series of events aimed at raising awareness of the benefits of welcoming immigrants, refugees, and native-born residents. In 2018, over 800 events were held across the country. On the welcomingamerica.org website, there are pre-translated signs and postcards to be used by participants, webinars to help host successful events, and a 'Welcoming Week Toolkit' which streamlines event planning by including sample activities, checklists, and press releases. By signing up on their website, event hosts gain access to promotional support, planning webinars and toolkits, marketing materials, and a cross-country searchable event listing. Welcoming America provides the opportunity for both hosts to gain the positive publicity of holding events and their communities to improve as environments for immigrants. The novelty of Welcoming America is that it has become a central resource center so that immigration reform can be approached from a unified front across the United States, focusing on each individual community rather than just larger metro areas.

Welcoming America's acknowledgment that a one-size-fits-all policy is oftentimes not the best approach—especially given the countless variables that go into proper reception of immigrants to their new community—has driven the movement's success. By essentially giving policymakers and civic leaders the opportunity to take what they need from the resources and base of information gathered, local leaders in each community have been able to maximize the preexisting foundations and values in their community rather than start from scratch. Just as immigrants represent a diverse range of cultures and countries of nationality, Welcoming America has allowed the United States to move toward accommodating these cultures in an inclusive way.

American Immigration Council

The American Immigration Council (AIC) is a nonprofit that has served as a "powerful voice in promoting laws, policies, and attitudes that honor our proud history as a nation of immigrants"(AICW). Since its establishment in 1987, AIC works to shape the American viewpoint towards immigrants and immigration and ultimately strengthen America by doing so. The core beliefs of AIC serve as a great foundation for their efforts (AICW):

- We believe that everyone deserves an opportunity to present their immigration claims in a fair and orderly way.
- We hold that our doors must be open to those who come to the United States in search of safety and protection.
- We believe that immigrants strengthen America by bringing skills, talents, and new energy to our economy.
- We believe in honest debates driven by the facts, not fear.

As the AIC website puts it, "through research and policy analysis, litigation and communications, and international exchange, the Council seeks to shape a twenty-first-century vision of the American immigrant experience" (AICW).

Aside from the largely legal focus of the AIC, they have programs in place which support immigrant introduction to communities and vice versa. One such program is their Cultural Exchange, through which the council sponsors internships at participating organizations across the United States. Many private for-profit and nonprofit organizations across the United States serve as hosts, and the AIC serves as the State Department designated third-party sponsor for J-1 trainees and interns. Essentially, the trainees and interns are recruited by the host organizations and then the AIC works with the organization to ensure it meets eligibility requirements as a host site. Once the host site passes the AIC screening process, they can then receive the interns or trainees with a J-1 visa. The entire AIC operation is associated with the immigration law community, which uniquely positions them to help with every step of the J-1 visa process because the AIC advisors are sensitive to attorney-client relations. The culture exchange advisors help immigration attorneys provide sound legal advice for their clients throughout the sponsorship process. Unlike the other two organizations mentioned, which call for welcoming immigrants after they have arrived in the U.S., AIC directly provides a route for immigrants to receive help during the immigration process.

AIC also contributes to the academic understanding of immigration. With publications such as "A Guide to S.744: Understanding the 2013 Senate Immigration Bill," "The Cost of Immigration Enforcement and Border Security," and "Facts About the Individual Tax Identification Number (ITIN)," the AIC is a resource for both immigrants and non-immigrant leaders seeking to better understand twenty-first-century American immigration. The legal foundation of AIC combined with the informational efforts sets the Council up for success in promoting immigration.

I Am An Immigrant

The I Am An Immigrant (IAAI) campaign, launched in 2016, centers around encouraging Americans to celebrate immigrants for their historic and ongoing contributions to society (IMMI). IAAI and **#CelebrateImmigrants** "encourages Americans to explore, celebrate, and take pride in their own immigrant heritage, and provides avenues for allies to stand in solidarity with their immigrant employees, colleagues, constituents, neighbors, and friends" (HACK). With partners such as Facebook, Squarespace, and Refinery29, IAAI is well-positioned within the media industry to gain traction for their movement. IAAI has an ongoing social media campaign under the hashtag #CelebrateImmigrants seeking to organize the voices and stories of immigrants in the United States to increase understanding of their presence and contributions.

Many of the events put on by IAAI are centered on Immigrant Heritage Month each June. The events include partnerships with organizations, religious institutions, and businesses. With events ranging from interactive public art installations in Salt Lake City to hackathons in Brooklyn, IAAI urges communities to come together and #CelebrateImmigrants. The Annual Immigrant Heritage Hackathon is dedicated to acknowledging the constant innovation necessary to welcome immigrants and ensure they have access to the resources necessary to contribute to their new homes.

The National Partnership for New Americans

The National Partnership for New Americans (NPNA) is a conglomerate of nonprofit pro-immigration advocacy groups. NPNA is a national, multiracial, and multiethnic partnership that represents the collective power and resources of immigrant and refugee rights organizations. Collectively, NPNA has a presence in 31 states and consists of 37 of the largest regional immigrant and refugee rights organizations. Member organizations directly provide services for their communities, ranging from health care enrollment to voter registration. In turn, the NPNA serves to leverage the collective power of the participating organizations and to provide expertise for a national strategy. The mission of the NPNA is based upon their shared belief that "America's success is rooted in our ongoing commitment to welcoming and integrating newcomers into the fabric of our nation, and to upholding equality and opportunity as fundamental American values" (NAPP). The strategy of the NPNA is to bring immigrant organizations vocal throughout the immigrant rights movement to the center of the national conversation about immigrant integration.

Programs of the NPNA are focused on the civic, economic, and linguistic integration of immigrants. The NPNA itself is not responsible for putting on the programs in each individual community but has participated in facilitating such programs through their training for "Community Navigators" and legal services. Community Navigators receive specialized training from the NPNA to provide quality immigration services and serve as "liaisons between their community, legal service providers, social service organizations, and government representatives." Initially, the Community Navigator training program was developed in partnership with the Committee for Immigration Reform Implementation, another immigrant rights advocacy organization. To date, over 9,400 "navigators" have been trained and tasked with educating their communities on rights, deportation defense strategies, and forms of immigration relief. Initial training for Navigators focused on deportation defense, Know Your Rights education, and naturalization work. As the climate surrounding immigration has changed, NPNA has adapted its training so that educators continue to learn information directly relevant to helping immigration in their communities. Training has been expanded to include local legal defense fund models, family preparation planning, and asset protection. Additionally, NPNA supports member organizations' efforts to deliver legal services to their communities. The NPNA network consists of over 26 organizations with legal capacity (meaning either the Board of Immigration Appeals Recognition or attorneys on staff). They also continually support members who are not yet Board of Immigration Appeals Recognized in their process towards recognition. Finally, NPNA directly holds immigration Law Training, which totals 40 hours in an effort to grow the legal service and training capacity in each community.

Conclusion

Especially given a political climate where divisions across party lines have muffled conversations about immigration, these nonprofits have kept the torch aflame in its time of need. These nonprofits have spearheaded multi-sided efforts, ranging from providing the necessary research on economic contributions to enabling grassroots organizations to host organized community events. Together, these approaches have led to the creation of communities that welcome immigrants as well as shifts in public opinion that have enabled immigrants to be successful as entrepreneurs and small business owners. There is a national awareness of the pro-immigration movement brought about by each of these organizations. The social change in support immigration is a demonstration of the importance of being proactive regardless of where an issue stands in Washington.

CHAPTER 11

A&A RELIABLE HOME HEALTH CARE

The path towards creating a successful small business is difficult no matter what, but entrepreneur Dr. Abraham Dalu progressed along this path while simultaneously uprooting his life to acquire an education and find religious freedom in the face of political turmoil. Dr. Dalu left his home in the Oromia region of Ethiopia after graduating high school in September of 1978. Unlike some immigrants who move directly from their nation of origin to the United States, Dr. Dalu's journey took a few detours. He initially moved to the former Soviet Union seeking higher education on a government scholarship because the Ethiopian government and the Soviet Union were aligned at that time due to the Ethiopian Civil War in 1974. After finishing his master's degree in the former Soviet Union, he fled to West Berlin by crossing the infamous Berlin Wall, whereupon he applied for political asylum in West Germany. At the same time, he heard that the United States was accepting applications from those who were coming from the Eastern Bloc, so he made sure to fulfill the requirements to be granted political asylum here as well. After applying at the American Consulate in Berlin and living in the city for nine months, his paperwork finally cleared and his application for political asylum was accepted. Dr. Dalu came to the United States at the age of 26 at the end of February 1985. As Dr. Dalu put it in our conversation, "and life started from there."

In the United States, Dr. Dalu did not immediately start his small business. He first returned to school for toxicology and then worked for multiple large corporations and federal laboratories. He worked in the pharmaceutical and biomedical research for many years while his wife, Aster, worked as a registered nurse for almost thirty years. After being fired in the third round of layoffs by his employer back in 2012, Dr. Dalu said he was "excited to have his destiny in [my] own hands rather than at the hands of corporations." Using his and his wife's health-based backgrounds and a desire to give back to the community, Dr. Dalu took being laid off as a blessing that enabled him to do what he wanted to do. In 2014, Dr. Dalu and his wife opened A&A Reliable Home Health Services, LLC. Upon opening the business, he was thrust out of his comfort zone of being successful in a corporate setting and into the uncertainty and responsibility of being a small business owner.

Despite home health care being a saturated industry at the time, the Dalus used their background, expertise, and understanding of the community's needs to propel A&A Reliable Home Health Services (A&A Reliable from here on) to success. A&A Reliable is a licensed, insured, and bonded "comprehensive home care agency" that offers 24-hour home health care services to patients. Services provided by the business include: "Supported Living Services, Home Care Nursing, Personal Care Assistance, Homemaker Services, and Independent Living Services." The Dalus do not treat A&A Reliable as a business, but rather as their vehicle to give back to the community. Regardless of age, nationality, and background, A&A Reliable services many senior citizens and disabled members of the community in Saint Paul, Minnesota. Dr. Dalu also emphasized the cultural considerations for clients. He ensures that employees have received culturally sensitive health education; he attributes awareness to this social responsibility as a contributor to the business's success. It is a particular strength of the business that they can cater to immigrant populations. In a conversation about building trust between clients and A&A Reliable health care workers, Dr. Dalu explained, "When they know that we understand their culture, we understand in some cases their language, it (puts us in a) position to respect who they are" (POSTY). As of the end of 2018, A&A Reliable had about 70 full- and part-time employees.

Just as A&A Reliable provides health services to the Twin Cities community, the employees delivering the care also need health care for themselves. Dr. Dalu previously did not have fifty full-time employees, so there was no health care plan in place for his employees. Given the small marginal profit of businesses in the home health care service industry, it was not financially attractive to his company to offer health care during its early stages of development. As he crossed the fifty full-time employee benchmark, however, he began looking into getting a company health insurance plan. His current health care hunt consists of conversations with brokers, looking at providers such as Medicare and Blue Cross, and searching for an attractive package. Even with the search for health care, he's unsure of how many of his employees will even have an interest in participating should he offer a group plan. The uncertainty arises because, for many of his employees, the hourly pay is not that much higher than the amount paid by the Department of Human Services (DHS) in the state of Minnesota where they are employed. Therefore, Dr. Dalu currently pays his employees the same amount as the reimbursement fee they would get from DHS. The Minnesota Department of Human Services is tasked with providing health coverage for low-income Minnesotans and for securing economic assistance for struggling families, including some of the employees of A&A Reliable (MNGOV).

Due to the fact that the amount the Department of Human Services reimburses is largely predetermined and he is confined by profits, he does not have the leverage to change the hourly pay; as a result, he believes many of his employees would not use a plan in which they can elect to participate because of the aforementioned reimbursement amounts. Further, many of his employees have already adapted to not receiving health care from A&A Reliable. Many employees are already on government-issued insurance, receive insurance from their primary job, or are covered by their spouse/partner who works elsewhere. Similarly, Dr. Dalu's wife still works as a nurse at a nearby hospital in addition to working at A&A Reliable, which covers the couple. Small business owners' uncertainty about the interest of employees in partaking in health care plans not previously offered is partially a reason why many approach the entire acquisition process with uncertainty.

A central consideration for small business owners is how much of the tax work is done in-house versus by a third-party company. A&A Reliable uses ADP for payroll, which has an online set-up where they help with hour tracking, payroll, giving employees payment checks, and ensuring that A&A Reliable has submitted the necessary documents to the federal government at the end of each year. ADP assumes the responsibility to provide Dr. Dalu with information about the ACA and health policy changes that affect his business. Dr. Dalu said that he appreciates having an external company keeping up with changes in Washington because it allows him more time to "focus on [his] business and growing it to its fullest potential." With the new health policy changes, Dr. Dalu acknowledged some financial uncertainty but remains optimistic about his health care acquisition plan.

An underlying theme of my entire conversation with Dr. Dalu was his humility and graciousness. When discussing being laid off, he expressed thanks for the corporation for giving him the opportunity to work there, accepting a new chapter of his life with no remorse or ill feelings. Similarly, when discussing their business, Dr. Dalu and his wife shared that the drive to give back to the community enables them to run the business with "passion and commitment." He was extremely candid about his immigration journey and shared a few thoughts about his perspective on immigration to the United States in general. Currently, Dr. Dalu is an active member of the Oromo Chamber of Commerce of Minnesota. This is another way in which he participates in his community as a business leader and empathetic individual.

Speaking those of the Oromia region of Ethiopia where he was born, he explained that he has observed many Oromos working in transportation, health care, and various nonprofit organizations and that they are doing "reasonably well." Yet, his ambition is not reserved only for his personal goals. He has hopes that the Oromo people take advantage of the educational opportunities in the United States to better understand how business works in the Western Hemisphere. He hopes that through the Oromo Chamber of Commerce, a relatively new group, Oromo businesses will be supported and able to achieve success in what they do. During his time serving as a member, the Oromo Chamber of Commerce has hosted productive meetings with various notable attendees, such as Minnesota state legislators. With the continued positive attention towards the Oromo Chamber, Dr. Dalu is confident it will set immigrant business leaders like himself in the right direction (MNMED).

As a member of the immigrant community, and more specifically as an Oromo immigrant, he is extremely attentive to the subtle changes that have occurred over the past decade. He thinks that "people are now getting out of the closet, and they are learning how the American political system works and how to be active participants in the process, which is the right thing to do" (MNMED). Through this awakening, he and his wife are able to both contribute to their communities and understand their rights as members of a community. This increased engagement has opened the doors in terms of education for immigrant children and access to public health services that may have been previously overlooked.

The success of Dr. Dalu as a minority business owner is tremendous considering the statistics for that region. According to the MinnPost, despite the fact that minorities represent approximately 22 percent of the Twin Cities' metro population, minority-owned businesses account for just seven percent of all firms. Both statistics for minorities and minority-owned businesses are relatively low compared to other metro areas such as Portland, St. Louis, and Cincinnati at 25 percent and 12 percent respectively. Unlike these metro areas that otherwise share many similarities with Twin Cities, its rate of minority business ownership places it along the likes of Providence, Rhode Island and Buffalo, New York.

Dr. Dalu believes that he shares a dream and a goal with his fellow small business owners. As a small business owner, he is proud to contribute to the economy of the state and the larger economy of his home country. On a more emotional level, he feels proud of the fact that he "did not let down the government that opened the door of opportunity to him to come into the United States." He also spoke to the perception that immigrants greedily take away from the federal government. In Dr. Dalu's case, he does not remember a single time since his arrival in the United States that he received any type of government subsidy. As an employee and employer, he has contributed taxes to both the state and federal governments. "I have been always living in the way of the true American dream. It makes me proud that I didn't squander the opportunity that was given to me. I realize that this only happens in America. And, also, it makes me proud that the risk I took to provide services to seniors and disabled individuals has led to the lives of other people improving. And that because of what I have started, other American and immigrants have gotten the opportunity of employment." Because of so many reasons he shared that, in a very humble way, he feels proud.

Printed in the United States
By Bookmasters